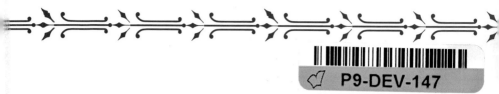

Wild West Women

Wild West Women

Travellers, Adventurers and Rebels

Rosemary Neering

Whitecap Books
Vancouver / Toronto

Note and photo credit abbreviations:
BCA British Columbia Archives
CVA City of Vancouver Archives

Edited by Elaine Jones
Proofread by Elizabeth Salomons
Cover and interior design by Graham Sheard

Printed and bound in Canada

Canadian Cataloguing in Publication Data

Neering, Rosemary, 1945-
Wild West women

Includes bibliographical references and index
ISBN 1-55285-013-7

1. Women—British Columbia—Biography. 2. British Columbia—
Biography. I. Title.
FC3805.N44 2000   920.72'09711   C00-911066-6
F1086.8.N44 2000

The publisher acknowledges the support of the Canada Council for the Arts
and the Cultural Services Branch of the Government of British Columbia in
making this publication possible. We acknowledge the financial support of the
Government of Canada through the Book Publishing Industry Development
Program for our publishing activities.

CONTENTS

ACKNOWLEDGEMENTS

My thanks go out to all the independent women I have met over my years of travelling the west. Prospectors, guides, hotel owners, wilderness dwellers: they contributed, without knowing it, to the background and insights that started me on this book.

Thanks, too, to all those who helped with the research for the book and who made suggestions or other contributions to the writing. Among them: Janet Blanchet, Veera Bonner, Elisabeth Duckworth (Kamloops Museum and Archives), Marlyn Horsdal, Audrey L'Heureux, Gillian Milton, Alice Mortenson, Bronwen Patenaude, Donna Redpath (Fort St. John-North Peace Museum Archives), Ruth Stubbs (Quesnel and District Museum and Archives), Rodney Symington (University of Victoria), Olive Torp, the staff of the City of Vancouver Archives (CVA), the staff of the Special Collections divisions of the University of Victoria and University of British Columbia, and the staff of the British Columbia Archives (BCA), particularly Kathryn Bridge, Dennis Duffy, David Mattison and Kelly Nolin. Thanks to editor Elaine Jones for her encouragement and support. And, as always, special thanks to Joe Thompson, who made concrete contributions to the research for the book and whose support was invaluable.

The author gratefully acknowledges financial support for the writing and research of this book from the British Columbia Arts Council and the Canada Council for the Arts.

Our Hearts Set on Adventure

Living in New York and hating it, Lillian Alling decided to walk home to Russia via British Columbia, Alaska and Siberia, and nothing—not exhaustion, not hunger, not a jail term—could deter her. Else Lübcke Seel turned against the tired old German literary world, came to Vancouver to marry a man she had never met, spent the next twenty-five years in the wilderness and had a ten-year correspondence with one of America's most notorious poets. Delina Noel could have lived in city luxury, but she was happiest using her prospector's eye and mining pick deep in gold country. Carrie Walker wasn't a prospector for precious metals, but mining men could be just as profitable as mining gold.

These aren't the women who built the west. Not nurses or teachers or crusaders for women's rights, they rarely show up in the history books, lauded for great political achievements. They are a different breed of women who often made their lives out beyond the cities. Adventuresome and rebellious, they strayed outside the permitted and undertook the unexpected. Imaginative, determined, often raucous, sometimes raunchy, they did what they wanted to do, regardless of others' disapproval. And what they wanted to do was run traplines, hotels or bawdy houses, prospect for gold, travel into and live in the wilderness, and marry as often as they wished or not at all.

They lived in an era informed by Victorian expectations of what a woman should do and who she should be. When American suffragette Susan B. Anthony marched into Victoria in 1874 and denounced the fact that women were not treated as equal to men, she aroused a storm of criticism, much of it from women who, in turn, denounced Anthony. "It is all foolishness, for we have plenty of rights now," wrote one woman. "We want no further rights. Our home is our palace, and in it we can find all that is necessary for our happiness." A male correspondent was a little hysterical in his fears: pass a bill giving a woman equal rights, he suggested, and the next thing you know she'll insure her husband and poison him with arsenic. "Under such a bill a woman could, with or without the consent of her husband, be at liberty to earn wages on the outside, either by artistic skill, shaming herself, or otherwise—and that, in the event of her earnings exceeding her husband's, she could, if she chooses, declare the marriage null and void." Not only that, women would start to engage in athletic sports, even going so far as tossing the caber, and "this would make her undignified and coarse."[1] A petition was presented to the government, signed by many of the prominent men of Victoria, saying a women's rights' bill must not be countenanced, for it would interfere with the sacred relationship between men and women, and make of lovely ladies weak imitations of men.

Introduction

In 1903, the *Atlin Claim* produced an article, poetic and pernicious, praising the ideal woman, who had no history and no story, was plucked from school before it was too late (much schooling seemingly being the destruction of the ideal woman), loved but did not reason, and while knowing that a man could love more than one woman, loved but one man herself.[2]

If a woman was married, she was expected to do as her husband bade her, to raise the children and see to the couple's social life. If, widowed or abandoned by a husband, or unmarried and not supported by her family, she needed to venture from the home to make a living, then she was generally limited to teaching, nursing or domestic service. While some women battled publicly against such expectations, and pointed out that poor women increasingly had to make a living outside the home and that middle- and upper-class women might expect the same, they were not a majority, and their definition of women's role in society was not widely accepted. Though attitudes and opportunities changed in the eighty years between the Cariboo Gold Rush of the 1860s and World War II, the woman who was adventuresome in 1935 aroused almost as much comment as the one who cast off society's expectations in 1865.

Most women who came to the west coast of Canada between the gold rush and the 1940s settled in Vancouver or Victoria, or in the growing towns in the interior valleys. Out beyond the cities, a different world existed. Along the coves and inlets of the coast, deep in the mountains of a dozen ranges, on the rolling hills of the dry country and among the lakes and rivers of the north, newcomers were exploring, prospecting for gold and homesteading. Even on the frontier, though, the expectation was that women would play the less adventuresome role centred on home and children. As a 1921 article on the Okanagan suggested, "Men's hearts were set on adventure, and if women followed somewhat reluctantly, they also showed great loyalty."[3] American author Julie Roy Jeffrey, writing about the role of women on the American frontier, found herself somewhat disappointed. "I had hoped to find that pioneer women used the frontier as a means of liberating themselves from stereotypes and behaviors that I found constricting and sexist. I discovered that they did not."[4] Instead, she found, women who went west took with them an ideal of feminine domesticity. Much the same held true for women coming to the Canadian west.

Recent books on the west, determined to give women their due, give an idea of how restricted was the role that women played in frontier society. The index entries for women in one such 1999 book of regional history read, *"childbirth; as governesses; medical skills of; as teachers; upper class; as wives of church officials; as wives of pioneers."*[5]

Yet there were women who were adventuresome, who did rebel. A few made their public mark: artist and writer Emily Carr is perhaps the best-known woman in British Columbia history and flamboyant newspaper editor Ma Murray had a coast-to-coast reputation. But most are not easy to find: the madam who plied her trade at the end of Main Street and the settler who dressed, cursed and smoked like a man rarely show up in local histories. Instead, they are found in a passing reference made by someone travelling through the region where they lived, someone who was impressed, shocked or amused by the lives they had chosen. They appear in newspaper articles written by reporters looking for the unusual. And many of them wrote their own stories, in unpublished diaries or published books.

Their adventures were relative to what their culture expected of them. Set up against the daily life of the native women whom she met, for example, Theodora Stanwell-Fletcher's initially clumsy attempts to deal with the realities of living in the northern wilderness were less than heroic, a fact she easily acknowledged when she noted that the native people they met suggested this was no life for a white woman, untrained and weak when compared to their own wives and daughters. For Stanwell-Fletcher, brought up in the much tamer environment of the American east coast, her seasons in the north were indeed an unusual undertaking.

+≡≡≡+

"I yell exultantly, 'All aboard for the Arctic Ocean and way ports!'" wrote Agnes Deans Cameron as she began her journey into what she called the Last West, "the last unoccupied frontier under a white man's sky."[6] Cameron, booted out of her teaching job in Victoria for being too adamant, too uncompromising, was one of a number of adventuresome women who found her destiny in travelling the west. "There has always been a West," she wrote. "For the Greeks there was Sicily; Carthage was the western outpost of Tyre; and young Roman patricians conquered Gaul and speculated in real estate on the sites of London and Liverpool."[7] Women travellers, consumed by wanderlust, found that journeying into the wilderness or reporting on the excesses of a raw new mining town gave them a freedom and satisfaction not to be matched in a settled and domestic life.

"I haven't just existed—I've *really* lived!"[8] wrote water-diviner Evelyn Penrose. Nonsense, she would have said, to the claim that women followed men somewhat reluctantly in the male quest for adventure. She bounced from place to place, always on the lookout for yet another exploit, whether it be proving that she could divine for precious metals, or discovering that native people had as many supernatural powers as she had and more besides. Other adventuresome women found their destinies in one location, setting up traplines, building cabins or tramping the mountains in search of gold.

Well-meaning acquaintances sometimes suggested that Chiwid should be confined to an institution, or in some other way restrained from her nomadic life as a wanderer, hunter and survivor in the Chilcotin—just as other well-meaning people put Lillian Alling in jail to keep her from what they saw as a hopeless and dangerous quest to trek north and ever farther west. Neither Chiwid nor Alling could be deterred: they were among the true rebels of the west. Like others, they ignored advice, suffered pain and invited rejection, yet remained unshakably on their own unusual paths.

What were they like, these wild west travellers, adventurers, and rebels? For any pattern that emerges, there are those who do not fit the pattern. Yet some common factors do appear. Many of these women were the daughters of strong, even domineering fathers—not altogether unusual in the Victorian era—whom they loved, hated and rebelled against in equal measures. In many cases, their fathers died when the daughters were still children or teenagers. Emily Carr, Evelyn Penrose, Gilean Douglas, Annie Rae Arthur: for all, the father was a central figure. "Perhaps it would have been all right if Daddy had lived,"[9] wrote Douglas many years after Daddy's death, forever a defining moment in her life.

Phyllis Munday did much of her mountain-climbing as an equal partner with her husband and Mattie Gunterman was married much of her life. They are examples of adventuresome women who lived in harmony with one male partner. But many more of these women were single, widowed, divorced—some several times—or of uncertain status. Emily Carr, for example, refers to the hotel keeper she met at Nootka as "just widowed on and off." Douglas and Rae Arthur each married four times; no one knows how many husbands Mrs. M.E. Allan collected and discarded as she ran her hotel in Rossland. Some women lived or travelled with a female companion. Some of these may well have been lesbians, practising or not, though that's much harder to decipher in records of earlier times than in the sex-obsessed decades after World War II. Whether from choice or from a lack of suitable husband material, it was not unusual then for a woman to remain unmarried: Cameron and most of her sisters, Carr and most of her sisters, were all resolutely single. Many unmarried women lived or travelled together, for

Many an independent woman had her photograph taken with the prey she had downed. Here, prospector, hunter and outdoorswoman Delina Noel poses with a bear that she shot. (BCA I-60887)

companionship, or safety, or because it cost less than living alone. Though some of these relationships may have been sexual, the majority were undoubtedly just the companionable pairings that they seemed to be. Only in the case of missionary Monica Storrs does a biographer hint at something more than friendship, perhaps because Storrs and her longtime female friend were buried in the same grave. Yet even Storrs spent much of her adult life on her own, away from this favoured friend.

Some women found it easier to rebel if they assumed the guise of a man. The *Rossland Miner* published a letter from a woman who could not find a decent job in that booming, brawling, 1890s mining town, so she decided to disguise herself as a man. Tall, weighing 165 pounds (seventy-five kilograms), she was, she thought, as strong and hard-working as any man. She pretended her long hair gave her headaches and had it cut off, bought a man's suit and went out and got a job that paid $2.50 a day. She drank a glass of beer in a saloon just to see what saloons were like—a freedom not permitted a "decent" woman—saved $200 over the summer, and planned to return to Toronto with her stake. "My advice to other young girls who are strong, hearty and young," she wrote, "is to do as I have done if they wish to get on in life. No one suspects that I am a woman."[10]

Much as the world loved to hear stories of their idiosyncracies, the stubborn and eccentric side of some of these women tested their families. Ma Murray's son was so exasperated by her conduct that he wrote an editorial in the family newspaper, disowning her. Jim Spilsbury reports of his mother, who wore men's clothing and lived in a tent, "Everybody we knew admired the hell out of her, but I hated to be around her. I would get so embarrassed."[11]

Introduction

Given the magnificence and variety of British Columbia's terrain, it is scarcely surprising that woven tightly into many of these stories is a surpassing love of the land. Distressed by her loneliness and her poverty, Else Lübcke Seel is ever buttressed by the beauty that she sees around her. "I love this piece of earth, every stone, every wave, rain and sun, ducks and moon,"[12] she wrote, a sentiment that is echoed by every woman who made her home on mountain, lake or rocky coast. Gilean Douglas found her paradise in the mountains and rivers of the Coquihalla country, Theodora Stanwell-Fletcher in the snows and silence of the north, Alice Jowett in the trails and mountains of the Lardeau. Perhaps there was something in the chaotic and majestic landscape that encouraged their desire to be adventuresome, to be rebellious.

Each one of them and many others chose their landscape, their place to counter the expectations of their times. They were the wild west women: travellers, adventurers and rebels, whose stories are this book.

Notes:
[1] as quoted in *Victoria Colonist*, July 11, 1976.
[2] *Atlin Claim*, May 9, 1903.
[3] Byron, LaVonne, "The Better Halves: The Way of Life and Influence of Women in the Vernon Area from Settlement to 1921," *Okanagan Historical Society Annual Report*, Vol. 45.
[4] Jeffrey, Julie Roy. *Frontier Women: Civilizing the West? 1840-1880* (New York: Hill and Wang, 1998), cover notes.
[5] Webber, Jean. *A Rich and Fruitful Land: The History of the Valleys of the Okanagan, Similkameen and Shuswap* (Madeira Park: Harbour Publishing, 1999), p. 238.
[6] Cameron, Agnes Deans. *The New North: An Account of a Woman's 1908 Journey through Canada to the Arctic* (Saskatoon: Western Producer Prairie Books, revised edition, 1986), p. 12.
[7] Ibid., pp. 2-3.

[8] Penrose, Evelyn. *Adventure Unlimited: A Water Diviner Travels the World* (London: Neville Spearman, 1958), p. 208.

[9] Douglas, Gilean. *A February Face* (unfinished autobiography in the Gilean Douglas collection, Special Collections, University of British Columbia).

[10] *Rossland Miner*, September 23, 1897.

[11] Spilsbury, Jim, and White, Howard. *Spilsbury's Coast* (Madeira Park: Harbour Publishing, 1987), p. 31.

[12] Seel, Else Lübcke. *The Last Pioneer: My Canadian Diary* (trans. Rodney Symington, unpublished).

Going for Gold

It was a cold and terrible winter that year on the Stikine River, and only fools set out overland through ice and snow to reach the gold diggings in the Cassiar. In December, two strong men experienced in winter wilderness travel had attempted the 160-mile (260-kilometre) trip, carrying provisions for eight days. Twelve days into their journey, they abandoned their sled and supplies and tried to turn back for their starting point of Wrangell at the river mouth. After twenty-two days in total, they stumbled into town, not having eaten for the previous five days.

It was clear that the journey should not be attempted before the weather improved. But you couldn't tell Nellie Cashman that. On January 28, the determined traveller, prospector and hotel owner set out on her own up the frozen river. The *British Colonist* of February 5, 1875, took up the tale:

> Her extraordinary feat of attempting to reach the
> diggings in midwinter and in the face of dangers

and obstacles that appalled even the stout-hearted Fannin and thrice drove him back to Wrangell for shelter is attributed by her friends to insanity. So impressed with this idea was the Commander at Fort Wrangell that he sent out a guard of soldiers to bring her back. The guard found her encamped on the ice of the Stickeen cooking her evening meal by the heat of a wood fire and humming a lively air. So happy, content and comfortable did she appear that the 'boys in blue' sat down and took tea at her invitation, and returned without her. It is feared that she has perished from the intense cold that prevailed during the latter part of January along the entire coast.[1]

Follow a mining rush in North America after 1870, and Nellie Cashman is there, running a restaurant, helping her fellow miners and, above all, looking for gold. She was far from the norm in the west. Through all the seeking for gold and silver—on the Fraser in 1858 and in the Cariboo through the 1860s, on the Stikine in 1861, on Wild Horse Creek below the Rockies in 1864, in the Omineca in 1869–70 and in the Cassiar shortly thereafter, in the West Kootenay and Atlin at the turn of the century, back in the Cariboo in the 1930s—it was almost always men who staked the claims, dug the shafts and set up and worked the placer, hard-rock and hydraulic operations that produced the precious minerals.

Government regulations actually prohibited women from working underground in coal mines from 1877 on, and from 1897 on in hard-rock mines. Cominco, one of the largest underground mining companies in the province, hired no women until 1974, and did so then only because of a shortage of male miners. The step required government permission, granted only on the proviso that the women have medical examinations every year rather than every two years, since the government had no data on how "lack of sunshine and high humidity" might affect women.

But there were always women who could not resist the lure of the precious metals that might be found in the bed of this stream, or that rock or that valley beyond the next mountain. Nellie Cashman was one of the best-known of these. Contemporary accounts about Cashman are contradictory. She was born in Ireland in 1844—or in the 1850s. She came to America with an aunt—or with a sister. She looked after the orphaned children of her sister from the time she was fifteen years old—or from her mid-twenties. She was blonde—or redheaded—or black-haired. It's certain, however, that she did come to the United States from Ireland, that she did support her nieces and nephews, and that she was about five foot three (160 centimetres), slight and consistently upbeat and merry. It's very certain that she was bitten early by the prospecting bug and that it never let go.

In 1873, Cashman heard stories about the silver rush to Nevada and headed out for Virginia City from the California coast, arriving in time to catch the tail end of the excitement—and perhaps meeting up with Martha Jane Canary, better known as the American frontier's Calamity Jane. In Virginia City, she opened a restaurant, and probably headed out when she could to do a little prospecting. By this time, though, there was little of the precious metal left to find. She and six other would-be miners, all men, found themselves in Pioche, near the Utah border—and Cashman got the nickname of Nellie Pioche. Discouraged by the lack of action, the group decided to move on to some other mineral rush. Would it be South Africa, where diamonds had just been discovered? Or would it be northern British Columbia, where a gold strike had been reported in the Cassiar country? A twenty-dollar gold piece was tossed in the air: heads for South Africa, tails for British Columbia. The coin came down tails.

In the summer of 1874, the seven-strong troupe arrived in Victoria, where they outfitted, then shipped out for Wrangell, on the Alaska panhandle coast at the mouth of the Stikine River. From Wrangell, they went upriver and overland to the Cassiar. In need of funds, Cashman opened a boarding house on Dease Creek, escaping whenever she could to prospect and pan for gold. She came down to Victoria with the other miners that fall; one of her first acts in the city was to send her mother $500.

Unwilling to wait for spring to return to Dease Creek the following year, Cashman ignored all advice and hit the

Prospector Nellie Cashman was young and still to achieve her name of "The Miners' Angel" when this photograph—one of the few in existence—was taken of her. (BCA D-1775)

trail in late January. But she confounded the doomsayers: on March 6, the *Colonist* reported that, despite more than fifty inches (125 centimetres) of snow, and temperatures that dropped below minus forty, Cashman was just fine. By that time, many miners and government men were headed in to the Cassiar; one traveller met "the famous Miss Cashman... on snowshoes and jolly as a sand-buoy. At the Boundary post she lost the trail and was 28 hours exposed to the pitiless pelting of a storm, without shelter or blankets."[2] She was, it seemed, none the worse for wear.

Cashman, usually the only woman in camp and certainly the only female miner, continued to attract attention from newspaper reporters. In a dispatch dated Dease Creek, July 17, 1875, the *Cariboo Sentinel* noted, "Miss Nellie Cashman, more familiarly called Nellie Pioche, is quite a character and deserves more than passing mention of her name. She kept a saloon and eating house here last year, and is said to have done very well. She was known to most of the Nevada miners.... She left Victoria with the first crowd of miners last February all alone; came up the Stickeen on the ice with her hand sled and 200 pounds of freight, in 18 days, with no companion only such as she met with on the trip, and since the middle of March has had her house open here doing all her own work."[3]

Cashman began to acquire a reputation as the "miners' angel." She gladly provided sympathetic words to sad or lonely miners whose claims did not prove out. She also was good for a grubstake for many a prospector heading out into the wilds. When she returned to Victoria in the fall of 1875, she noticed that St. Joseph's Hospital was under construction. The next season on the Cassiar, she collected from the miners and sent the money back to Victoria for the hospital.

Her legend also declares that she took vegetables and lime juice over the treacherous trail in midwinter when she heard that a group of miners was starving—but the same stories insist that the trip from Wrangell to Dease Lake took her seventy-seven days, an implausible length of time.

"She had an amazing personality," said an article written at her death, "with a sunny smile and most infectious laugh, which won her friends wherever she went."[4] Slight as she was, Cashman seemed to have no fear of the wild country she delighted in, or of the men who surrounded her. She declared that she never carried a gun, and wouldn't know what to do with one. "At one time for two years I was the only white woman in camp," she told a reporter years later. "I never have had a word said to me out of the way. The boys would sure see to it that anyone who ever offered to insult me could never be able to repeat the offence.

"The farther away you go from civilisation, the bigger-hearted and more courteous you find the men. Every man I met up north was my protector, and every man I ever met, if he needed my help, got it, whether it was a hot meal, nursing, or whatever else he needed."[5] But Cashman didn't let her affection for men go too far. She never married, saying that she had no desire to look after one of the "boys" for life, convinced as she was that men never really grew up.

By the end of 1876, Cashman and her fellow miners were bound for other rushes, other mother lodes. Silver had been found in Arizona and Cashman set out for Tombstone. There she stayed for a number of years, running restaurants and hotels, grubstaking miners and finding a little time to do her own prospecting. Her reputation for charitable works grew as she gave time, energy and money to such things as the building of a hospital.

But for anyone with the gold bug, there's always another rush, another reason for the excitement of moving on. In 1883, the *Colonist*, which kept track of her, noted that "Miss Nellie Cashman, who was one of the original prospectors of Cassiar, went back to Lower California with a party of gold prospectors a short time ago. She just got back, having come near dying of thirst in one of the deserts. They found placers, but they were worked out a year ago."[6] In 1898, she headed north again, this time lured by the great gold rush in the Klondike. As she passed through Victoria, the *Colonist* noted the arrival and departure of this "lithe attractive looking woman with jet black hair [who] possesses all the vivacity and enthusiasm of a young girl. Her personality is very striking, and her experience in mining matters...to say the least has been unique."[7]

Cashman described to the reporter how she dressed when on her expeditions. "In many respects as a man does, with long heavy trousers and rubber boots. Of course, when associating with strangers I wear a long rubber coat. Skirts are out of the question up north, as many women will find out before they reach the goldfields."[8]

In the Yukon, Cashman ran the CanCan restaurant and staked claims, with the restaurant rather more successful than the claims. In 1904, she left Dawson, lured farther west by a gold rush in Fairbanks, Alaska, where she started a grocery store and went prospecting once more. Three years later, she continued down the Yukon River, on a raft with an old sourdough, headed for the Koyukuk district. Here she remained for almost twenty years, declaring that her mining claims were the farthest north gold property in North America. By the 1920s, now in her seventies, she decided that she needed more capital if she were to develop her claims properly. She went outside, to Seattle, but had little success raising money. Three years later, now probably near eighty, she ran 750 miles (1200 kilometres) from Koyukuk to Seward by dogsled, a trip noted matter-of-factly by the Seward newspaper: "In from Koyukuk, Thanksgiving night, 17 days out of there by dog team, came Nellie Cashman…. From the farthest north mining camp to New York City is her trail trip this time, and any obstacles that surmount the trail between here and New York might just as well get out of the way for she's hit the trail and is going through."[9]

It wasn't to be. She caught a chill, and had to go to the Anglican mission for care. From there, she was taken to Juneau and on down the coast to Victoria. In that city, she walked into St. Joseph's Hospital with pneumonia. She died in the first week of January 1925. She is buried in the Ross Bay Cemetery in Victoria, her grave marked by a simple stone.

At the age of ninety-three, Alice Elizabeth Jowett took her first airplane ride. There was no doubt in her mind about where she wanted to go: from high above her beloved Lardeau mountains, she looked down on the mining claims she had staked many years before.

Born Alice Elizabeth Smith in the Yorkshire city of Bradford on a stormy night in 1853, she took up the baking trade as a young woman. In 1878, she married Thomas Jowett, and they had four children. Within ten years, she was left a widow. Eschewing the clamour of industrial England, she was drawn instead by the glamour and promise of adventure to be found in western Canada. She welcomed challenges: instead of taking the route now normal to the west coast, by steamer and train, or even the still arduous but

Alice Jowett, centre, would never leave her beloved Lardeau, in the West Kootenay, where she prospected and ran her hotel. In this photograph, she is surrounded by Revelstoke Board of Trade members in front of her famed Trout Lake City hotel. (BCA B-00036)

relatively safe trip across the Isthmus of Panama, she and her children boarded a sailing ship in 1889 and set out for the newly fledged city of Vancouver by way of Cape Horn, at the far southern tip of South America.

In Vancouver, she opened a bakery, which she operated for seven years as her children grew up. But Vancouver's Cordova Street, different though it was from Bradford's Manchester Street, did not hold the adventure she was seeking. In 1896, hearing the stories of gold and silver to be found in the Arrow Lakes region of the West Kootenay, she moved with her family to the Lardeau area, settling in the raw, new and hopefully named town of Trout Lake City.

Fewer than 500 people lived in Trout Lake City, but the mining boom brought prospectors, gamblers and entrepreneurs of all kinds, enough to support five hotels, a water system, a branch bank, two general stores, a telephone system, a hospital, sidewalks, a newspaper and a stage line to Beaton, on Upper Arrow Lake to the west. Jowett bought the Trout Lake City Hotel to ensure herself a living, and transformed the log building from a mining camp saloon into a fine hotel.

She soon attracted customers. She bought a second hotel, the Windsor, a three-storey frame building overlooking the lake, complete with bar and billiard room. There, she established hotel-keeping standards she was to sustain for all of the fifty years that she was in the hotel business, through Trout Lake City's inevitable collapse once the mining excitement dwindled and the rushers moved on to other speculations. The Windsor was famed throughout the region for its roast beef and Yorkshire pudding, Irish linen tablecloths and silver cutlery. Jowett was equally known for her standards for staff. Years later, one woman who had been employed at the Windsor as a young girl recalled that her employer could be demanding: "I made tea one day and she said the water wasn't boiling. She picked up the pot and threw it across the yard."[10] But Jowett was also quick to defend her girls if advances were made or arguments occurred. Few customers transgressed again once they had felt the impact of those bright blue eyes and cutting words.

Keeping a hotel was her job. Prospecting was Jowett's love. Not long after she arrived in Trout Lake City, she was riding the hills on horseback and walking the trails, seeking promising gold and silver claims. On a ridge near the summit of a nearby mountain, she staked the Foggy Day, the Arralu, the You and I, the Alpine and the Hercules. More interested in the thrill of discovery than in the exploitation, she then leased the claims to others. In later years, she sold one of her claims for $20,000.

Not that Jowett was afraid of hard work. Interviewed the day before she turned 101, she looked critically at the young woman reporter. "You ought to get wider shoulders," she advised. "I used to use dumb-bells and Indian clubs. I used to have great muscles. I worked and I wasn't afraid of it."[11] She wasn't afraid of enjoying herself either. As a young girl, she had begged her father to allow her to perform in opera but he refused. She loved music all her life and would still break into joyous song when she was in her nineties.

By 1900, the mining excitement had died down, and the Lardeau was settling into silence. The prospectors who had signed the Windsor's guest book in days past—from places like Rawhide Trail and Rabbit Creek, Horseshoe and Nickel Plate—no longer came to town for rest and recreation. The number of guests from all around the world dwindled. But Jowett was resolute: Trout Lake City was her home and there she would stay. She visited her claims, hiked the hills, rode horseback out though the forests and "went out" to mining conventions elsewhere in the West Kootenay and in Washington State.

Her mining expertise was well respected, both at these conventions and on her home ground. "It sounds unbelievable," recounted a friend, "but Alice doesn't have to look at a sample of ore to tell whether it is gold, silver, or base metal—she simply smells it and she knows."[12] Like many another dreamer of El Dorado, Jowett claimed to have found a "mystery mine," the source of crystal flowers set with gold, diamonds and other valuable minerals, samples of which she said she sent to Ottawa. She never revealed the mine's location.

She was ninety-two when she took her last horseback ride. At ninety-three, she went up in an airplane to survey her mining claims. At ninety-nine, admitting that she had lost a step because of her rheumatism, she moved into a seniors' home in Kelowna, in the Okanagan Valley, where she liked the sunshine but missed the Lardeau. In March of 1955, she died there, coherent till the last day, when she slipped into a coma.

Wrote ghost-town historian Bruce Ramsay, "If any one person can be singled out as representing the spirit of the mining camp, that individual would be Mrs. Jowett. She never gave up hopes that the 'boys would come back again,' and for all the years that she operated the Windsor, until 1945, the dining tables were always set, laid with a complete setting of silver and the crispest of linen."[13]

"Oh, how I loved that country," she declared at the age of 101. "I loved the trees and the mountains and the lake full of fish at the foot of the hotel."[14] Alice Jowett went back to the country she loved one more time. Her ashes were taken to Alpine Basin, in her Lardeau mountains, and buried beneath a cairn of rocks from one of her mining claims.

❧❦❧

Minnie Mead May cared more for her mine than anything or anyone else in her life. Little more than five feet (150 centimetres) tall, speaking with a soft Virginia accent, brought up to be seen and not heard, she seems the least likely of people to carry on a vigorous and protracted court battle. Nonetheless, she spent thirty-eight years in and out of court, trying to regain ownership of the Gibson silver-lead-zinc mine near Kaslo.

May led an adventuresome life from the time she was a young girl. She told people that a voice in the air had revealed her future husband's name to her when she was five years old and sitting under a locust tree, already wondering how to get to the California she had heard people talking about. She met David May when she was sixteen, followed him to California and married him soon after. In 1916, the Mays headed out to British Columbia and went prospecting in the West Kootenay. They found a silver-lead prospect that they liked twelve miles (nineteen kilometres) from Kaslo, bought it and raised $85,000 through the sale of a million and a half shares. Three years later, they were offered $2 million for the property, now called the Gibson mine.

From here on, the tale is obscure. Someone else, with shareholder backing, incorporated the Daybreak Mining Company, even though the Mays said they still owned most of the original shares. They first went to court to get back possession of the Gibson in 1919. In 1932, they apparently won title, but somehow neglected to get a court order for possession. Back to court Minnie May went, again and again: Court of Appeal, Supreme Court of B.C., Supreme Court of Canada, even the Privy Council in the United Kingdom. Minnie May fought most of these battles on her own. In 1920, David May suffered a nervous breakdown brought on by the dispute and went back to live on their farm in Montana, where he died in 1955.

Surrender was not in Minnie May's vocabulary. She lived in small Vancouver hotels, toting her trunks of legal documents—and her books on astrology and palmistry—from hotel to hotel when she was forced to move by circumstances or poverty. Wrote a Vancouver reporter in 1953, "Drawing herself up to her full five feet in height, her blue eyes flashing fire, she says: 'I'll fight, I'll fight to the end of my life if necessary…because I know I'm in the right.'"[14] She spent almost all her time on her battle, writing letters, putting together evidence compiling the material in her briefcase and trunks into long screeds for her court cases.

Minnie Mead May died on Christmas Day, 1957, still convinced that she was right, the participant in one of the longest-running court cases in Canada. Given her belief in reincarnation, it may not be over yet.

Other women ventured into prospecting and mining, though most did so part-time and with their husbands. Mrs. George Petty was working with her husband one summer day when the heat felled him, and he had to go home. Working on, Petty found the first traces of ore in what would become the Victor mine in the West Kootenay. She was a tough and tall woman, "as capable of digging pits as her husband. She used to come to town in britches and high boots with a big pack sack. She was always potting bears— she wasn't afraid of them at all."[15]

Mining entrepreneur Viola MacMillan bought the Victor mine for $65,000, and later said she made more than $10 million from it. The daughter of an Ontario farmer, MacMillan met and married George MacMillan, a prospector's son in Ontario, and opened a boarding house while her husband tried out life as a junior stockbroker. But her interest in mining grew and she persuaded her husband to quit his job and go prospecting. For twenty years, they hunted for gold and other precious metals in northern Ontario and Quebec, and in the Northwest Territories. Then they came to British Columbia, where they had no luck, often finding it difficult to make the ten dollars a day they needed to keep going. They were considering bailing out when Viola learned that the Victor was for sale. With no money, the MacMillans floated stock to raise cash, then eventually bought the stock back with the profits from the mine.

Said the *Chicago Tribune* of her, "Perhaps remembering that she had walked over a good part of Canada before she struck it rich, Mrs. MacMillan watches over her property with all the attention that a hen gives its brood. On most days she can be seen standing at the entrance to the ViolaMac base metal mine, her own private Fort Knox, which projects from a mountainside nearly five thousand feet above a remote valley. It is one of the biggest lead-zinc producers in Canada.

"Mrs. MacMillan's daily routine parallels that of her miners. She lives in a decrepit one-room shack near the mineshaft and takes her meals in the camp cookhouse with the hired help. A small attractive woman, nearing fifty, she handles a diamond drill or pick with the best of them and often teaches novice miners the tricks of the trade."[16]

⊹⟞⟝⊹

"Can women mine in the Cariboo?" asked the *Vancouver Province* of June 17, 1933. Perhaps they could, concluded the article; in fact, one woman had indeed staked a claim in the new 1930s gold rush on Williams Creek. But there was a paucity of women in the old Barkerville, said the writer, and the Cariboo had never appealed to women settlers. "In the mines," the writer said, "life was rough and hard, and there were few attractive occupations open to women." But perhaps times had changed: "Milady's surprising eagerness for adventure and not-so-surprising empty purse" in those depression days might "urge many of the previously hailed 'weaker sex' to pull on oilskins and rubber boots and enter the gold fields of Cariboo — not as decorative dancing partners, nor as helpmates, nor even as housekeepers, but as serious competitors of all male miners. Perhaps a 'Golden

Daisy,' 'Betty Money,' or 'Barkerville Kay' will replace 'Cariboo Cameron' and 'Twelve-foot Davis' as bonanzas of Cariboo."[17]

The 1930s in Barkerville did not throw up any famous women miners, but to the southwest, near where the dry country meets the coastal forests, Delina Noel was chipping away at rock and making her claims to mining fame.

Back in the 1860s, Québecois farmer Joseph L'Italien Laventure crossed the Rockies and rafted down the North Thompson River with the large contingent of gold rushers known as the Overlanders. Laventure continued on to Barkerville, but, like many of the Overlanders, he didn't stay: too many hopeful men, too little gold. He retraced his steps south, and started a ranch near Lillooet, the original starting point of the Cariboo Road. In 1879, French Joe, as he was known, went back to Quebec to marry a school-teacher. The couple returned to the ranch, where they had two daughters. By 1883, they had sold their ranch to the government and returned to Quebec, where their daughters went to school. Laventure came back again in 1895; in 1896, his wife and daughters arrived. Not long after, daughter Delina, then twenty, married a local prospector and miner, Arthur Noel.

Almost her first act as a married woman was to go by pack train from Lillooet by way of high mountain lakes and passes to Noel's mine. She wasn't welcome. The men working there, imbued with the superstition that said no good could come of a woman at a mine, immediately threatened to quit if Delina stayed. Arthur stayed firm: Delina would have the same privileges as any man in inspecting the work face. She gradually became a welcome visitor, and a worker. By 1902, she was the superintendent of a 10-stamp mill that

processed the gold ore. Though she was never an underground miner, she was "top man" in a shaft-sinking project,
and in 1909 she carried her own gold brick to the assay
office in Vancouver. During World War I, when many men
left to fight in Europe, she went to Vancouver to recruit new
miners: the five she hired were all considered excellent.

She studied geology assiduously and staked her own
claims in the area of the Noels' Lorne mine, one of the best
in the Bralorne region. The fireplace in the Noel cabin was
made from samples of the rocks of the region, some ore-
bearing, some simply of interest to Delina. She claimed a

Prospector Delina Noel and friend Louise Brampton pose at a small
mining operation in the Bralorne country west of Lillooet. Though
the Noel claims and mines made her a prosperous woman, she
preferred prospecting in the back country to living in the city.
(BCA I-60886)

fraction of land that had somehow escaped staking. When she sold it, it became an important part of the very profitable Bralorne mine. In 1929, claim jumpers knocked off a fifteen-cent padlock she had used to secure the wooden roof of an exploratory shaft she had sunk, and took over a claim. She won the claim back in court; her list of costs included the price of the padlock, now vastly inflated.

She quickly became both hunter and trapper. One story tells of the time a huge grizzly reared up over husband and wife. Both shot; the grizzly toppled, an 800-pound (360-kilogram) beast almost ten feet (three metres) tall. She tended traplines in winter, bringing in lynx, rabbit, fox and coyote, and once bartered a fox pelt to a prospector in return for his mineral claim.

Delina Noel continued to explore, prospect, hunt and trap throughout the 1930s and 1940s. In 1946, Arthur died — and Delina outfitted six old miners with new suits, so that they could carry the coffin. She tried life in a Vancouver house bought with the Noels' earnings from their mines and claims, but she was soon back in the wilderness, spending her winters in a house in Bralorne, her summers prospecting. "She scorns the city and a life of ease," ran a *Vancouver Province* story in 1947. "She spends the good weather months hunting for precious metal in the rocky, treeless crags that look down on the Pioneer, Bralorne and the gaunt timbers of heartbreak prospects. They say she can pack 30 pounds all day and break rock or cut wood with the best of them."[18]

Reporter Art McKenzie caught up with Noel at her prospector's cabin on a creek near the fabled Lorne and Bralorne mines. That day, Noel had been more than 1,700 feet (500 metres) up the mountain; her trouser pockets were full of rock samples. She unlaced her mountain-climbing boots, served her guest water with a little lime juice added and talked a bit about her day. But not much: Noel wasn't interested in revealing herself to reporters, and she turned down a number of would-be biographers. Many guessed at how much money she and her husband had made from their claims and mines, but Noel would never say. Nor, burned at least once by claim jumpers, would she ever say precisely where she was prospecting or for what.

When she died in 1960, the small, grey-haired woman was hailed as B.C.'s most illustrious female prospector and mine developer, well-respected in the industry and closely listened to when she went to mining conventions. In 1958, British Columbia's centennial year, Delina Noel was told that she was to be presented with a plaque recognizing her contributions to the mining industry of B.C. At that time, she was hard at work developing a copper-tungsten prospect high in the same pass she had followed with that pack train as a newly married woman. She came down to Lillooet for the presentation, but it was a close call. Delina Noel would rather have stayed in the mountains, working her claim.

Notes:

1 *Daily British Colonist*, February 5, 1875.
2 *Daily British Colonist*, March 6, 1875.
3 *Cariboo Sentinel*, July 17, 1875.
4 *Vancouver Province*, January 17, 1925.
5 *Victoria Colonist*, January 11, 1925.
6 *Daily British Colonist*, June 13, 1883.
7 *Victoria Colonist*, February 15, 1898.
8 Ibid.
9 as quoted in *Vancouver Province*, January 17, 1925.
10 Parent, Milton. *Silent Shores and Sunken Ships* (Nakusp: Arrow Lakes Historical Society, 1997), p. 235.
11 *Kelowna Courier*, November 4, 1954.

[12] Ibid.

[13] Ramsay, Bruce. *Ghost Towns of British Columbia* (Vancouver: Mitchell Press, 1963), pp. 115-116.

[14] *Vancouver Province, BC Magazine*, November 29, 1953.

[15] Farrow, Moira, *Nobody Here but Us: Pioneers of the North* (Vancouver: J.J. Douglas, 1975), p. 91.

[16] *Chicago Tribune*, 1953.

[17] *Vancouver Province*, June 17, 1933.

[18] *Vancouver Province*, October 4, 1947.

I SPENT THE NIGHT IN MY VALISE

Travelling with Notebook and Sketchpad

Forced into the United States by the vagaries of the British Columbia transport system in 1897, Frances Macnab knew to expect the worst. Americans, she had discovered, were rude, crude and frequently lewd. Always in a hurry, they could be expected to be dishonest, and a lone woman risked her honour, if not her life. When she reached Bonners Ferry, Idaho, having rejected a trail ride alone since she did not wish to be robbed or murdered—or both—"to gratify the greed of a cowardly desperado," she was horrified at the accommodation she was offered, particularly the shabby excuse for a bed.

But such minor mishaps could not daunt a stalwart Englishwoman, a writer who had travelled the dominions on her own. She unrolled her sturdy and useful Wolseley valise, and shook out her kaross (a skin garment she had presumably picked up on her South African travels). Thus prepared for the night to come, she left the room for a spot of river fishing.

Macnab—the pen name used by Agnes Fraser—took the reader along on her journey through British Columbia, by train, horse, steamer, dugout canoe and on foot. On this particular evening, as horrified by what the dining room offered as she had been by the bed, she bought a steak, made her way to the river, lit a fire and broiled her meat over the ashes. Then she sat on her cloak watching the fire and drinking tea until she judged the time right to fit together her fishing rod, climb aboard an old hulk moored by the bank and cast out into the riffles of the river.

It was a beautiful and peaceful scene, improved by a chat with an old Indian who drifted by in a bark canoe just as she

Frances Macnab had all her suspicions about Americans confirmed when she was robbed near Grand Forks, at the American border. This photograph shows the border crossing the same year that Macnab travelled through the region. (BCA A-03698)

struck a fish. The owner of the hulk came aboard to shoot ducks with a shotgun. A passing woman invited Macnab to her house, where she regaled the writer with tales of the American south. Macnab then returned to her hotel. "I spent the night in my valise," she wrote, "and breakfasted the next morning on boiled eggs, making my own tea..."[1]

Macnab was one of many writers who travelled through Canada after the completion of the CPR to Vancouver in 1886. Several things set her apart from the others. She had written travel books on other countries and would proceed to write more. She did a thorough research job that extended to more statistics than anyone might care to know. A woman travelling alone in a field that was mostly male, she loved fishing and would throw a line in at any moment of boredom or respite. She was perhaps the quintessential female traveller of the British Empire: independent, convinced of the supremacy of almost all things British and undaunted by difficulty.

Macnab began her book with a summary of British Columbia's history. Unhappy that such a fine British province should be populated partly by Americans, she commented, "They are a people prepared for anything, because they have nothing and are greedy to be rich, loving both wealth and the pursuit of wealth, till the value of everything is gauged by dollars and cents.... They are a people composed of the restless dissatisfied fractions of many nations."[2] She was equally scathing about the rush for Klondike gold then just beginning. No good would come of it, she warned; it would depopulate British Columbia of its fine young men—and not so fine older men—who would die or return to live with shattered constitutions, unable to farm or otherwise build B.C.

She came across Canada by train, courtesy of the Canadian Pacific Railway. Near the Rocky Mountains, miles of track had been twisted out of shape by a washout and hastily repaired. Together with her fellow passengers, she descended from the train, edged across rails to which boards had been lashed and suspended just above the Bow River, and climbed aboard a freight train on the other side. Astonished by a large crate which the railwaymen were loading, she asked if that might not have awaited another train. Not at all, replied the men; it was a coffin, carrying the bones of a Chinese man who had died in Canada. It must arrive in time to be shipped from Vancouver on the *Empress of Japan.*

Impressed by her first sight of the Rockies, comparing their "wild ferocity and sharpness of outline"[3] favourably with her own rounded Essex hills, she was nonetheless irritated: this was the sort of scenery one should be alone with, and oh, for a horse, so that she might ride away into the mountains. Macnab continued on by rail and steamer to Victoria, where she was impressed by the city's natural setting, but disappointed by Vancouver Island: "no money, no markets, the water supply a disgrace and a menace to health.... If the people of Victoria exerted themselves to render the town attractive to residents, Victoria might have a future."[4]

On she continued to Alberni, commenting that Chinese men made far better immigrants than the English, since they possessed persistence and industry, two qualities sadly lacking in Englishmen. "The great defect in the British emigrant is his unadaptability, and many men would be useless in any but one capacity, while others appear to regard a change of occupation as degrading."[5] She got in a little fishing at Sarita, near the mouth of Alberni Inlet, disembarked from the small and crowded steamer early and gloried in at last being alone and able to gaze her fill at the great Douglas firs as she walked the two miles (three kilometres) to Port Alberni, then was dismayed to discover that being late for breakfast meant that she got none. But a woman who has crossed Africa and North America does not easily accept the word *no*. She obtained a "clammy poached egg, which was not very fresh, a glass of milk and some excellent white bread." [6] Then she started upriver with two men in a canoe and her fishing rod, only to find that British Columbia salmon would not take a fly in the river. She had to content herself with several small trout and two larger ones. "I caught the two largest fish with a fly which I tied myself for bass fishing"[7] in England.

The next morning she mounted a horse in deplorable condition, and took a moment to decry the brutality with which westerners treated their horses. But she could not walk the fourteen miles (twenty-two kilometres) to the Alberni mines, and consoled herself with the supposition that, if she did not take the horse, someone else would, and would treat it worse. The forest on the way to the mines impressed her mightily, with its 600- to 800-year-old trees, up to eight feet (2.5 metres) in diameter, 300 feet (100 metres) high. No other forest could compare, not that in England, nor that in Africa.

Next, she continued by stagecoach to Nanaimo, whose wretched and poverty-stricken miners did not impress her at all. Two Indians took her south by dugout canoe. To get more money from her, they staged an "accident" that took them onto the rocks, but she stood firm, the canoe was repaired and all set off again in good humour. Though the scenery was grand, she was somewhat bored, so out came the fishing rod again, trailing a line with a spoon bait behind the canoe.

Macnab continued on to Victoria, then across the Strait of Georgia and up the Fraser River. This journey took her to New Westminster, Harrison Hot Springs, Chilliwack and on foot up and down the farm fields in the vicinity. Throughout, she gathered facts and figures and expectations for the country, all of which she explained to the reader. She also expounded at great length on training the young and making the country grow. By train, on foot, by stage, by boat, Macnab toured interior British Columbia from the Okanagan to the Kootenays. Never tactful, she expressed her opinion firmly. The smelter town of Trail, with its mean, sordid and depraved housing and people and odiferous fumes, was a veritable blot on the face of nature. Rossland, on the other hand, was a cosmopolitan town infinitely more pleasant than such mining towns as Johannesburg.

All were marred by the presence of Americans. Though at one point she insulted Germans, Jews and Americans with the impartial prejudice of a Victorian Englishwoman, Americans were the most annoying. They expressed great impertinence and impudence towards Great Britain, despite their own high crime rate, flagrant immorality and unbelief. The times when she had to go through the United States in order to continue her trip brought great misery. And then, arriving from Spokane in the Canadian town of Grand Forks, she was robbed of her purse.

"As I got down from the stage amongst the most evil-looking set of scoundrels I ever saw in my life, I believe it was taken from me then."[8] But it was useless to appeal to the police, she said; with the many stages that passed through at all hours, anyone who wanted to evade the police simply put on the dress of a miner and moved on.

She travelled back and forth from the U.S. to the Kootenays, happily fishing wherever she could. At one point, camping by the side of a stream, she pulled off her shoes, stockings and skirt to wade out to where she saw a trout rise. She caught the fish, but could not recommend the experience. "I had some way to walk to reach my shoes, and approached them in an attitude of adoration—typical, I thought, of the mental condition in which I rejoined the C.P.R. whenever ill-luck separated me from it for any length of time."[9] But a hot cup of tea and a trout cooked on the coals of her fire soon restored her spirits. She then invited a couple from the nearby town to her camp, cooked them a fowl "African fashion" and moved on once more.

The remainder of her trip took her up and down the Columbia Valley by steamer, on horseback and on foot. We see her last, sitting alone on that oh-so-useful valise, in a travel-stained suit of jungle cloth and a battered straw hat, waiting for a steamboat that would connect back to the C.P.R. tracks, a train to Banff and Quebec and a ship to Liverpool—and on to more adventures in the Empire.

Macnab was not the only Englishwoman to chronicle British Columbia. She differs from many of the others, however, because she came here specifically to write a book. For others, a book was the incidental result of a trip undertaken for other reasons. Lady Hariot Dufferin, for example, travelled with her husband Lord Dufferin while he was Governor General of Canada from 1872 to 1878, later publishing *My Canadian Journal*.

Like Macnab, Lady Dufferin was an inveterate fisherwoman, rising at dawn on many an occasion to test the waters of stream or lake. But, as befits the consort of a royal representative, she was much less judgmental of what she saw along her way.

She spent a week in Victoria in 1878, then continued up the coast to Metlakatla, stopping to fish and hunt at various coastal settlements along the way. The Queen Charlottes she characterized as "the wildest place that I shall ever be."[10] She also visited New Westminster, saw a water performance by Indians carrying torches in their dugout canoes and continued up the Fraser by steamer to Yale, whence they embarked on the Cariboo road by stagecoach. They went fishing at Kamloops, then returned south, with Lady Dufferin riding on the box of the coach most of the way.

The year after Frances Macnab railed against the effects of the Klondike Gold Rush, Faith Fenton bushwhacked through northern British Columbia, ready to report on the Klondike. For the early years of her writing career, Fenton was a mild-mannered school teacher by day, an intrepid journalist by night. Born Alice Freeman in a small Ontario town in 1857, she was one of seven children in a thirteen-year span. When she was ten, her family, overwhelmed and impoverished, sent her to live with a childless clergyman and his wife. Though the exile from her family was wrenching at the time, it gave her many opportunities not available in her genteelly poor birth family. Her new guardian was better off than her old family; she was affectionate and helpful with her new charge; she was also a poet who encouraged the young girl to write. But, four years later, the woman who had taken the place of her mother died, and she returned to her original family.

Freeman/Fenton then took teacher training. She taught school for nineteen years. In the midst of this career, she took on another. She began to write for newspapers, taking at first the pen name Stella—for respectable women still did not become journalists, and teacher Alice Freeman could not be known as one such—and then the name of Faith Fenton.

Fenton freelanced for various Toronto publications for a number of years. In her summer vacations from school, she often travelled through eastern Canada, writing about what she saw. Her columns on women's role and women's rights, couched in careful language so that they would be printed in newspapers whose editors were not particularly supportive, won her a large and loyal following, both in Toronto and in the Canadian west. Finally, in 1894, she took the plunge. She left her teaching job to write full time.

For a few years, she did well. She was probably Canada's first woman magazine editor, taking on the task for the *Canadian Home Journal*, launched in 1895. Then she lost that job and saw no prospect of another that would pay her a living wage. Return to teaching? Not a chance. Fenton decided instead to go to the Klondike, earning her keep by sending back articles describing this great gold rush.

In British Columbia, we see her first in Vancouver in 1898, where she arrived with a four-woman contingent of the newly formed Victorian Order of Nurses, also Klondike-bound. The nurses and Fenton planned to go north with the 203 men of the Yukon Field Force, a military corps sent to show the Canadian flag in the Yukon and to let Americans know that the Klondike was not in Alaska, as so many of their newspaper reports would have it. In her kit were two dark green mackinaw cloth suits, with a daring skirt that came just to the knee, to be worn with bloomers. A proponent of Rational Dress for women, Fenton was convinced, and rightly so, that longer skirts would be a hindrance on the rough, muddy and difficult trail they proposed to follow. But the short skirts would raise some eyebrows en route, and she would have to hastily tack on an extra piece of material, to hide her legs for as long as she was in the town of Wrangell. She also took with her heavy boots, a summer-weight suit, a blouse with many pockets, a long heavy cotton overcoat— and a long raccoon coat, presented to her by the Hudson's Bay Company in Vancouver. The *Victoria Colonist* was sure that Fenton would add to the group: "she…possesses a faculty of being of assistance and adding life to any party,"[11] noted the reporter of the woman who was known to be outspoken, well-spoken, enthusiastic and often very funny.

The group headed north to Wrangell by steamer. From there, they set out on an all-Canadian route—necessary for a Canadian military group—up the Stikine River by steamer, then overland on the barely broken trail that led north to the Yukon. Nurse Georgia Powell commented that only the "strongest and most sinewy women" could have tackled the trail, which began with a few miles of railway grade, then continued ever narrower and rougher along Telegraph Creek and over a 4,000-foot-high (1200-metre) pass.

Writer R.M. Patterson years later described what the rest of the trail must have been like in 1898. "Down into the dreary muskeg country," he wrote of their journey, "leaping from log to log, bending the willows flat to make some kind of footing, wading up to the knees in the muskegs, with the frost as the only solid thing to walk on. How they did it passes the imagination," and Patterson here is talking about the men of the field force. "It would have been bad enough for one or two men alone with a mule or two. But with a mob like that, churning the trail to sludge, and with millions of mosquitoes on the war path…the mind reels at the thought alone."[12] They were not alone on this poor excuse for a trail: some 10,000 people passed through Glenora, below Telegraph Creek on the Stikine River, in 1898.

Fenton focussed on these and the other people she met along the trail, refusing to describe the difficulties she must have encountered for her readers back east. She sent back word pictures of a plucky woman she met on the trail and described with humour the small tent she slept in and the horse she sometimes rode. She found, as many independent women were to do, great joy in the country through which she passed. "Oh the lovely aloneness of it all," she wrote, "so far away from men and women and bricks and newspapers."[13]

The trek as far as Teslin took them almost three months. At the lake, the military men built the scows and rowboats that took them the final 400 miles (650 kilometres) to Dawson City, "down unknown lake and river, through shoals and eddies, currents and rapids, to the golden Canadian northland."

Fenton had not planned to stay in the Yukon but the rapidly advancing winter overtook her. She was contemplating how she could make money to survive—doing laundry perhaps, or cooking—when she met a young doctor named John Brown, who was serving as secretary to the dominion minister of the interior, then likewise on a visit to the Yukon. Brown had read and admired Fenton's columns back in Toronto. As Fenton settled into Dawson City society, sending back dispatches to Toronto and finding a job as editor of the new newspaper, *The Paystreak*, the friendship between the two developed. They were married in Dawson in January of 1900. As the rush wound down in 1904, they left Dawson, planning that this would be just a sojourn "outside."

They never returned. Though Fenton wrote less and less, she still contributed the occasional freelance article to newspapers and magazines. She died in Toronto in 1936.

+·——·——·+

The photograph of Julia Henshaw shows her wearing a rather Grecian garland twined about her head. There's something of the society woman that Henshaw was in the photograph, but also something of the adventurer: draped across her chest are the medals she won in wartime France. Missing from the picture is her life as a writer, traveller and sometime botanist. What also does not show is the bitterness her energy and dispatch caused at least one rival.

Henshaw was born Julia Wilmothe Henderson in England in 1869, the daughter of reasonably well-off parents, her father an ardent amateur naturalist. As a young girl, she travelled with her father to the continent, and went to school in both France and Germany. Her arrival in Canada isn't documented, but she must have been just barely out of her teens when she came to Montreal, for by 1890, she was married with an infant daughter. Her husband, Charles G. Henshaw, had all the right connections. He was of United Empire Loyalist stock, his brother-in-law general manager of the Bank of Montreal.

In about 1891, the Henshaws moved to Vancouver. Charles, better known as Charlie, doesn't seem to have made a great impact in Vancouver social circles, though he had something of a reputation as a practical joker. A man who visited Julia in the 1930s commented in a letter to the brother-in-law, "It would seem that Charles was gone; perhaps he was dead,"[14] an intimation that his comings and goings were of great interest neither to Vancouver nor to his family.

Writer Julia Henshaw wears the decorations she was awarded for service in France in World War I. Henshaw wrote, travelled and sought adventure until illness slowed her down. (CVA Port.P.1073, N 943)

The couple were noted as adventuresome travellers and Julia made a name for herself as a society hostess. In 1896, it was reported, admiringly, that they had reached the sources of both the Kootenay and Columbia rivers. Presumably, the report was made by someone who did not know that the two rivers are very close indeed. But Julia's real interest was in writing. In 1898, the publication of her first potboiler novel was greeted with fulsome praise: "The book of the year as far as B.C. is concerned is *Hypnotized*, the new novel by Julia Henshaw. The story is likely to give the author, at once, an acknowledged place among the most graceful writers on this continent. The story has probably not been surpassed by any yet written in Canada."[15]

Two more novels followed. *Why Not Sweetheart* was based on Henshaw's own travels in the B.C. interior through the West Kootenay into Rossland. In it, the evil Professor

Panhandle, a maiden's worst nightmare, receives his come-uppance and love triumphs over evil—though one of the fine male characters does not survive that triumph. "The blood spilt by that brave man of Strathcona's Horse will help keep Canada forever green in the heart of the British Empire," reads the ending of the novel.[16]

Possessed of tremendous energy, Henshaw freelanced while her daughter was young, then took on a full-time job from 1900 to 1910 as editor of the Sunday page in a Vancouver newspaper. During that time, she founded several societies and became a member of others; she also travelled widely in British Columbia, indulging her passion for mountain climbing and for botany. Her research in the mountains led to the publication of *Mountain Wildflowers of America* in 1906, a seminal book with descriptions and photographs of ferns, grasses, trees, rushes and flowers.

Botanist, mountain climber and fellow writer Mary Schäffer Warren never forgave Henshaw for that publication, which appeared a year before Schäffer's own painstakingly compiled and illustrated mountain wildflower guide. A year or two earlier, Henshaw had visited the town of Field, where Warren's first husband, Charles Schäffer, was botanizing. She asked many questions about the plants of the region and about the techniques of illustration and photography that Mary Schäffer was pioneering. Like many a serious—and slow—scientist pre-empted by a speedier journalist, Schäffer Warren was outraged by Henshaw's tactics. Cyndi Smith, chronicler of women who climbed and worked in the Rocky Mountains, noted that "Mary frequently ranted about a certain party getting the F.R.G.S. (Fellow of the Royal Geographical Society) by showing MY slides at the Royal Geographic Society."[17]

It's unlikely that Schäffer Warren's annoyance affected Henshaw. She continued to write and to climb. In 1910, her article on mountain climbing in Canada, in the *Overland Monthly*, detailed, in somewhat flowery language, her expedition with famed Swiss guide Edward Feuz and a companion to the top of Asulkan Pass at 7716 feet (2352 metres). She headed out on a pinto horse, in her thin flannel shirt, tweed knickerbockers and short wide shirt that was comfortable enough to climb or ride in. Her strong, nailed boots reached to her knees, a soft silk tie was knotted around her throat, and a pair of Indian buckskin gloves protected her hands from mosquito bites, sharp rocks and ice pinnacles: at times, the reader is not sure whether this is a society woman discussing fashion or a serious mountain climber. A broad-brimmed felt hat was fastened with her Strathcona's Horse badge of which she was very proud. She took with her a woollen sweater, a folding Eastman Kodak camera easy to use on the climb, a pair of field glasses and a pair of blue goggles, to protect her eyes from the glare.

The trio completed the climb. Securely roped between the two men, Henshaw gaily attacked the steep slope of the glacier. A photo shows her, jaunty with her ice axe. At the top of the pass, they indulged in sandwiches, fruit and chocolate brought along in Feuz's rucksack, then drank some melted snow with a dash of cognac from a collapsible cup. The wind kicked up and down they went.

That article was published in 1914 as war broke out in Europe. Charlie Henshaw set up in Vancouver's Victory Square as recruiting officer for Vancouver, working out of a tent. At first, Julia was content with helping her husband and giving speeches and raising money for the war effort. But soon she was overseas with an ambulance and food unit.

She was mentioned in dispatches for her courage and was awarded the Croix de Guerre with gold star for her work in evacuating several towns that were under enemy shellfire and aerial bombardment. At some point, presumably after the war when it would have been possible to transport such a gift, the French government presented her with a mammoth painting of Napoleon, which hung, somewhat out of scale, in her West Vancouver house.

In 1920, the French Alpine Club hosted an international Alpine Congress in Monaco. Julia Henshaw was there, lecturing on the flora and fauna of the Rocky Mountains, her lecture illustrated by hand-coloured lantern slides. From about that time on, Henshaw was in poor health and did little more writing, hiking or climbing. But she had achieved some measure of fame for both her writing and her actions. An interviewer who visited her in 1932 was much impressed and matched her own style to Henshaw's rather purple prose. "She has scaled the heights in search of beauty which grows near to Heaven, and she has traversed the road that leads in the opposite direction, through the ugliness and horror of war-torn areas; drawing rooms, and...pomp and ceremony...courage and a desire for knowledge of the untrodden ways have been hers."[18]

Henshaw died in West Vancouver in 1937, at the age of 68.

Emily Carr was the most famous of the women artists who set off independently to depict the country from the Rockies to the coast. Norah Drummond Davies garnered much less fame as she painted scenes of mountains and wildlife, then lived out the rest of her life on Vancouver Island. In her later days, Drummond Davies was well known on the streets of

Victoria, striding forth in her dark wool skirt and short grey wool jacket with ample pockets—and, except when the weather was just too warm, a bushy-tailed coonskin cap.

Drummond Davies, born in 1862, came to Canada from England between the two world wars. Already well known for her commissioned series of paintings of hunting scenes, she was sent to Banff to paint Canadian wildlife. For five years, she lived in a log cabin on the mountainside, doing first-hand research into the animals that lived in the wilds. She had with her two Airedale dogs that she attached to a light cart in summer, a sleigh in winter, driving them over the trails in the Banff area. "Everyone in Banff knew the sturdy figure dressed in mannish attire," wrote a newspaper reporter in the 1960s, "and her team of dogs. They dubbed her 'Little Casino'—a name by which she is still remembered up that way today."[19]

Short, sturdy, tanned, with bright brown eyes and short dark hair streaked with grey as she grew older, in summer she rode horseback, using a stepping box that she kept tied to her saddle horn to help her mount and dismount. Fifteen of her paintings, scenes of wildlife and native life, were displayed in Calgary in the 1930s. Among the collection were paintings of a bear watching a trout stream, Rocky Mountain sheep, a mountain lion creeping down a defile to his prey, a grizzly bear, a herd of cattle swimming a mountain river, and a buffalo herd—surely not done from life, since Drummond Davies did not reach the west until after the great herds of buffalo had been killed off.

Her wildlife-painting completed, Drummond Davies moved to Vancouver Island with her Airedales, living in a cabin near Sidney, north of Victoria, and travelling in her dog-drawn cart with paints and brushes. The dogs aged and finally she had to shoot them. But she acquired new dogs and moved into Victoria. When that area got too crowded for her, she moved west of the city, into another isolated cabin, coming into town once a week for supplies. She died in 1949, at the age of eighty-six, another of the independent women chroniclers of the west.

Notes:

1 Macnab, Frances (Agnes Fraser). *British Columbia for Settlers: Its mines, trade and agriculture* (London: Chapman & Hall 1898), p. 320.

2 Ibid., p. 321.

3 Ibid., p. 5.

4 Ibid., p. 165.

5 Ibid., p. 175.

6 Ibid., p. 183.

7 Ibid., p. 188.

8 Ibid., p. 280.

9 Ibid., p. 319.

10 Dufferin, Lady Hariot. *My Canadian Journal,* Gladys Chantler Walker, ed. (Toronto: Longmans Canada, 1969), p. 209.

11 as quoted in Downie, Jill. *A Passionate Pen: The Life and Times of Faith Fenton* (Toronto: HarperCollins, 1996), p. 241.

12 Patterson, R.M. *Trail to the Interior* (Victoria: Horsdal and Schubart, 1993), pp. 101-102.

13 as quoted in Downie, *A Passionate Pen,* p. 254.

14 Dwoemy to Williams-Taylor, June 5, 1928, Vancouver City Archives.

15 *Vancouver Province,* December 8, 1898.

16 Henshaw, Julia. *Why Not Sweetheart* (Toronto: George N. Morang, 1902), p. 246.

17 Smith, Cyndi. *Off the Beaten Track: Women Adventurers and Mountaineers in Western Canada* (Jasper: Coyote Books, 1989), p. 58.

18 *Vancouver Province,* June 13, 1932.

19 *Victoria Times,* August 24, 1966.

A SURPRISING GRASP
OF BUSINESS AFFAIRS

The Hotel Women

Said the judge to Pansy Mae Stuttard, "Were you pointing the rifle at the police constable?"

Said Pansy Mae Stuttard to the judge, "If I had been, he wouldn't be here—and neither would I."

Case dismissed.

Outspoken, eccentric and successful, Stuttard was a 1920s inheritor of a long tradition of feisty women hotel owners and saloon keepers that began in 1850s Victoria and extended past World War II. On this occasion, Stuttard, the owner of a hotel in Delta, south of Vancouver, was engaged in one of her many skirmishes with the law. The law, in the person of a deputy police constable, said she had pointed a rifle at him. Stuttard claimed innocence: she carried the rifle to protect the young goats she raised against predatory eagles.

Stuttard had had a long and varied career. A New York nurse, she worked for the Red Cross, travelling to the

Philippines, Cuba, Mexico, and Central and South America. She told a reporter in 1951 that she had arrived with the first contingent of U.S. troops in Cuba, spent six years bringing fever patients from Panama to the United States during the building of the Panama Canal, and nursed in the Spanish-American War. In 1905, she moved to Vancouver, where she met and married a British naval officer. The two started a small fleet of tugboats to ply the coast, and Stuttard worked as a mate for three years, then became the first woman to obtain a coastal waters master's ticket, travelling from Vancouver to Alaska and occasionally going ashore to resume nursing duties.

In the 1920s, her husband deceased, decamped or dismissed—the record doesn't say—she built an inn with sixteen rooms and dance floor close to the United States border, hoping to profit from U.S. residents who were suffering under Prohibition. The move didn't make her particularly popular with Delta residents—but then, the overly moral Deltans weren't too popular with Stuttard, who suggested the region had too many churches and too few people. Nonetheless, she was forced to give up plans for a cabaret, and to call the building a lodge, not a hotel. For some reason, the police were not convinced of her pure intentions, and frequently dropped by to check the place out and lay charges. Accused on one occasion of keeping liquor, she claimed she did not know that one of her guests, a brewery representative, had ninety-one sacks of beer in his room. This charge, too, was dismissed. In 1936, Stuttard closed her lodge and tore it down, saying she was getting too old to argue with the law. She built instead a large water-front home in Tsawwassen, then moved later to White Rock, where she died in 1963.

The Hotel Women

The keeping of a hotel or boarding house was one of the respectable—or sometimes, semi-respectable—occupations open to a woman who wished to venture into frontier country. It was also one of the more lucrative possibilities, since the population in every boom town was more or less transient, and the demand for rooms high. It provided an income and a position for the woman who wanted to go prospecting or who found the city too confining. Many a mining town hotel, roadhouse along the way to mining rushes or boarding house was owned and run by a woman.

One of British Columbia's earliest and best-known hotel and saloon keepers was Madame Fanny Bendixen. Some say she was the mistress of an underworld figure in San Francisco, but gave up her furs, gold and wayward life to marry Louis Bendixen and flee from her ex-lover's revenge north to Victoria. There, the Bendixens opened the St. George's Hotel. Traveller Walter Cheadle commented, when he returned from the hardships of his trip to the Cariboo, "We reached Victoria at 6.30 & went to St. George's where we were rapturously welcomed by Mrs. Bendixen. Had bath & went to theatre where we saw tragedy of Camille, a version of Lady of Camellias, much overdone by Mrs. Dean Hayne." With some irony considering Bendixen's girth in later years, she "inveighed against the degradation of (Cheadle's) dining with 'le gros boucher'" the mayor, Thomas Harris, who weighed 300 pounds (135 kilograms).[1]

By the mid-1860s, Victoria had more hotel rooms than would-be guests, and the St. George's went bankrupt. Louis Bendixen went back to California—though he showed up again in Barkerville later—and Madame headed for the Cariboo. Once she reached Barkerville, she claimed to have been the only woman to have packed in all her own gear over the rugged trail from Quesnelle Forks. She settled in on main street, and somehow raised the money to open a saloon in June of 1866. "Parlor Saloon, Barkerville," ran her advertisement. "Madame Bendixen begs to announce to her friends that she has refitted this well known Saloon, where she invites the public to give her a call. The bar is stocked with the best of LIQUORS and SEGARS that can be procured."[2]

Like some other women hotel owners, Bendixen soon got herself involved in a lawsuit. In 1868, she took a man named Portnam to court, to obtain possession of a one-half interest in a mining claim. The newspaper report does not

Men gather outside Madame Fanny Bendixen's hotel in Barkerville, in gold-rush days. The portly Fanny required two chairs if she wished to sit down. (BCA C-09314)

say on what basis Bendixen made her claim but she lost the case. Four months later, she also lost her hotel. The fire that ravaged Barkerville in late September of 1868 destroyed the saloon, at a cost of about $5,000. She took on a partner, and they rebuilt on the lot she owned; she continued on as hotel and saloon operator for many years. As late as 1889, Judge Matthew Baillie Begbie noted that "Madame Bendixen is here in great form, indeed enormous, vast, of undiscoverable girth, though she was always of goodly diameter."[3] At some 300 pounds (135 kilograms), Madame now needed two chairs if she wanted to sit down. She died in 1899, her age unknown.

Barkerville's women hotel owners and operators were a sometimes rowdy lot; perhaps they had to be to compete with men in this most rowdy miners' town. Eliza Ord showed up in town in the 1860s with a man who may or may not have been her husband. She soon discarded him, withdrawing the power of attorney she had given, and opened the Cariboo Exchange Hotel in 1867. "No expense has been spared to render the House all that could be desired for comfort and convenience,"[4] her advertisement declared, and the *Sentinel* pronounced the hotel equal to anything in Victoria.

To open the hotel, she had fought something of a battle. A few months earlier, Ord announced in the *Sentinel* that contrary to reports from "certain malicious persons," she was indeed the hotel's sole owner, and anyone who cared to could have a look at the title deeds. Sadly, the hotel burned in 1868, and Ord lost $10,000. Out of business, but not out of energy, Ord showed up ever more frequently in court, arguing sometimes as defendant, sometimes as plaintiff, over the ownership of mining claims, property damage suits and proofs of ownership. She broke all the windows in the house of another Barkerville resident, though why is still unknown.

The suit that provided Barkerville with the most gossip was one for breach of promise. In the early 1870s, Ord was keeping company with Robert Drinkall, described as a man of means and comparative wealth. Ord said that Drinkall had promised to marry her whenever she wished, but that two years later, he had refused to marry her, thereby breaching his promise. Drinkall and Ord had lived together, and Drinkall had paid out money to support her. Some said that Ord had a general reputation as an unchaste woman, while others vigorously denied the allegation. One man was reported as testifying that "the plaintiff's reputation was that of being a chaste woman, and if he had known or heard anything to the contrary he would not have gone near her house."[5] Another witness agreed: "with the exception of the time she was living with Mr. Brooks, I am not aware by rumour that she cohabited with anyone else."[6] The defence declared that "the action originated in fraud and was supported by effrontery and falsehood."[7] In an odd twist of legal argument, the defendant's lawyer claimed that there had been no agreement, because Ord was not bound to marry Drinkall; and if there had been an agreement, it had been ended when Ord brought suit. "Her sole end and ambition was money, and the defendant had been her dupe.... Her general character was so bad as to justify any sane man in breaking such a contract."[8] While several witnesses declared that Ord had a creditable character, another said she was a bilk and a privateer, a woman sailing under false colours. She lost the case.

She left and returned and left and returned, always involved in controversy. In 1889, she sued over a mining claim, accusing a judge of taking money from the claim. She was adjudged insane and shipped off to New Westminster. But New Westminster begged to differ.

"A woman named Elizabeth Ord was brought down from Barkerville by Constable Lindsay," read an article in the *Vancouver World*, "on the plea that she was insane and a fit subject for the lunatic asylum, where it was intended that she be domiciled for an indeterminate time...[the doctors here] declared her to be sane. Accordingly, she has been liberated, and will be allowed to return to her home in a few days. It appears that the medical men in New Westminister differ in opinion from their fellows in the upper country."[9]

Janet Morris, also known as Scotch Jennie, provided a contrast to Fanny Bendixen's girth and Eliza Ord's temper. Morris set up a boarding house in 1862; Walter Cheadle was much impressed. He noted meeting "Janet Morris, a Scotchwoman, fair, fat & forty, the wife of a man who keeps a store, & who came to make the plum-pudding &tc., & of course sat down & dined with us."[10] He and his companion Lord Milton were doubly charmed when Morris presented Milton with a twenty-five-dollar gold nugget for him to give to his mother. One of fewer than a hundred people to winter in Barkerville in 1862, she was one of just seven women to do so.

Husband Morris died, and Jennie married William Allen. She operated the Pioneer bar and hotel at Mosquito Creek, near Barkerville, where, it's said, she once let two miners throw dice to win all of her stock of wines, paying an ounce of gold per bottle. From that wager, she netted some $1,500. Scotch Jennie was known for her kindness: she cared for sick miners, and once, the story goes, walked through deep snow for several days to reach a sick man.

On a Saturday late in August of 1870, she drove her carriage along the narrow road through Blackjack Canyon, on the way to Barkerville. The carriage crashed into the rock wall on the left, then tumbled into the canyon on the right, and Jennie was badly injured. A hundred miners, reported the *Cariboo Sentinel*, rushed to the canyon to rescue her, bringing her back to Kelly's Hotel. At first they thought she had suffered only a broken leg, but two days later she died of internal injuries.

"A large number of people attended the funeral," reported the newspaper. "Miners from Lightning and other creeks stopped work and came to Barkerville to see the last of poor Jeannie. The banks and nearly all the stores in Barkerville

"Maw" Allan's sturdy hotel was the first brick building in Rossland, a tribute to her business skills if not to her somewhat confusing marital life. (BCA B-04981)

were closed during the funeral. Mrs. Allen came to Cariboo in 1862 and acquired the respect of every one by the numerous acts of kindness she performed in cases of sickness or distress. Whenever any accident occurred or in any case of serious illness she volunteered her services and became the nurse and friend of the miner.... All the flags in Barkerville were hung at half-mast, and all the circumstances and solemnity of an extraordinary funeral were exhibited."[11] Less charitably, but probably with equal accuracy, it was reported as well that she "dressed like a man, drank like a man and died like a man."

Over in Rossland a few years later, Mrs. M.E. Allan was raising eyebrows. Allan came to B.C. from Ontario, living in Vancouver, then opening a hotel in Nakusp, then moving on to boomtown Rossland. The Hotel Allan was one of several opened by women in that town's explosive gold rush years. Allan (known as Maw) built one of the first of Rossland's after-the-shack-stage buildings, a $4,500 hotel on a main downtown corner. It opened in August of 1895 with a grand ball. A Mrs. Lewis opened another hotel in September and a Mrs. Shaw yet another in October. Mrs. Lewis opened a second establishment in 1896. The first brick building in Rossland opened as the Hotel Allan in 1896–7.

"The Hotel Allan," ran its description, "is the pride of Rossland and par excellence the best hotel of the British Columbia gold fields. It is the tourists' resort, the commercial travellers' choice and a first favorite of the travelling public.... The Hotel Allan embraces two fine modern buildings, one of brick. It was designed and built with especial reference to its fitness for a first class hotel suited for this climate. The house occupies one of the best business corners in Rossland and is a popular place of resort for capitalists, mining men, financiers and business men of the city."[12] Its eighty-five large guest rooms and wide hallways were lit by electricity, its hundred-seat dining room magnificent, its bar and card rooms the finest in the city.

As for Mrs. Allan, she "has personal charge in conducting her hotel, assisted by experienced clerks, stewards and efficient help in every department. Beside her hotel business, Mrs. Allan has valuable mining interests and is developing some mining properties.... Mrs. Allan has manifested a grasp of business affairs both gratifying and surprising to her friends. She is a lady of education and culture, of graceful manners, with the ready and tender sympathies of a mother and a tact and judgement in business affairs unusual in her sex."[13]

The prideful history doesn't mention another of Allan's attributes. According to Walter McRaye, who toured with Pauline Johnson in the early 1900s, Allan had had more than one husband. "Mrs. Allan loved 'em and left 'em. She would slip across the border to Spokane and divorce each when tired of him. It was said that two or three of her ex-husbands were working around the place."[14]

Women were not always welcome in the hospitality trade. Englishman Harry Cole ran the Greyhound Hotel in infant Vancouver around 1887–88 and brought in young women from England to serve in his hotel. Given the shortage of marriageable women in the area, it's not surprising that most soon left his employ to get married. But when another hotel tried the same thing during the Klondike Gold Rush, the employment of women was equally short-lived—though for a much different reason. "Although Vancouver in the Klondyke period was pretty much 'wide open', these later barmaids were a little too tough," wrote a newspaperman in the 1920s, "and were quickly ordered to give way to the masculine barkeep."[15]

Boom towns were good places for women who wanted to run hotels and who weren't too fussy about the conduct of their clientele. Popcorn Kate ran a bunkhouse at Log Cabin, a settlement between the White Pass and the gold rush town of Atlin in 1898. One night, she staged a wine-drinking contest, entry fee a dollar. A hose was attached to a huge cask of wine, and the contestants took a swallow and moved to the back of the line; the last man standing was the winner. No one remembered who won. Kate moved on to Atlin, and ran the Discovery Hotel there. Atlin historians say Kate herself was the main attraction, with a ready ear for miners' troubles. But like one or two others in Atlin, she ran into difficulty with a liquor licence and moved on to more hospitable towns.

On her travels along the west coast, Emily Carr encountered a fine example of the rough-mannered hotel owner. When she visited Nootka in 1929, she stayed at a ramshackle waterfront hotel, "a long narrow frame building that straddled a gulley there was a door at one end and the approach to the door was three planks elevated on stilts. The hotel was run by a woman with a girl child of six, maybe the woman was wholly a widow, maybe not, maybe she was just widowed on and off...."[16]

The hotel, wrote Carr, offended every one of her five senses, but her indignation peaked when the woman stood up in the dining room and announced that no food would be served the next day, because she was going off picnicking. Serve yourselves from the larder if you want, said the woman. The next morning, Carr found her tea and toast rather better made than usual, prepared by a fellow guest, who commented on the flies in the room, then said he would cook them a steak dinner that night. The meal was good, but Carr was still annoyed at the manager's casualness in the running of her hotel. "Well," said the man, "she is a casual piece, but good enough at heart.... Home runnin' ain't in some wimmin. Ye jest carnt lern 'em."[17]

Others, probably the majority of women hotel owners, found they took to the running of a hotel, a job that gave them independence and a degree of freedom. Dora Homan and Grace Stanton arrived in Quesnel, in the Cariboo, in 1910. Clearly imbued with the desire for adventure, they had left their home in the United States to visit the Seattle World's Fair in 1909, then continued north, to work at the hundred-room, four-storey Occidental Hotel. Homan took over the dining room, where she grew a maze of plants that reached to the ceiling, among them ferns, begonias and even, it is said, a blue rose that survived through the winters. Fire destroyed both the Occidental and Quesnel's other hotel in December of 1916. Some of the men fighting the fire ran to save Homan's plants, but she dissuaded them, for the plants would only freeze once taken outdoors.

Seeing the opportunity occasioned by the loss of both Quesnel hotels in the fire, the women set up in business for themselves, opening a boarding house that they called the Stan-Hom Lodge. This they ran until 1925, when they leased the British American Hotel. When that hotel was sold, they went back to operating the boarding house.

Stanton was known as a botanist. The women maintained a backyard garden, where they experimented with walnut trees, different varieties of apples and such things as melons and grapes. Though Homan helped out in the garden, she grew ever more interested in the supernatural.

Dora Homan (seated) and Grace Stanton, her business partner and longtime friend, ran hotels and boarding houses in Quesnel, where Homan gained a reputation for her psychic skills, and the pair for their gardening innovations. (QUESNEL AND DISTRICT MUSEUM AND ARCHIVES)

"I know I am psychic, I was born that way," she wrote in one of her notebooks. "When I first started to predict happenings, people did not believe me, but when they came true, people sat up and took notice of what I said."[18] She was also an astrologer and spent much time casting horoscopes for an increasing number of clients who consulted her about their lives. A night person, she sometimes stayed up through the night casting horoscopes.

An avid reader, Homan was a fan of Agatha Christie mysteries and collected books on such topics as cosmic vibrations, moon signs and the cause and cure of cancer. She and Stanton were known as pack rats: to enter their premises through a narrow corridor lined with boxes filled with all manner of memorabilia was a challenge. When Homan's diaries arrived at the Quesnel Museum and Archives, they were an equal challenge, written on scraps of paper, cardboard, and even toilet paper. Grace Stanton, some years older than Homan, died in 1941. Homan continued to live in Quesnel, and died in 1964 at the age of eighty-five.

Not every hotel woman was aggressive or eccentric. Myrtle Phillip, with her husband, Alex, built the celebrated and pioneering Rainbow Lodge at Alta Lake, just south of the present town and ski resort of Whistler, and ran it for almost thirty-five years. Alex came west from Maine in the early 1900s; Myrtle, who had met him when she was fifteen years old, came out to marry him in 1910, when she was nineteen. The next summer, they took a boat up Howe Sound to Squamish, then a stagecoach up the valley that extended northwest. When they reached Alta Lake, surrounded by mountains and virgin rainforest, they fell in love with the land.

For two years, they visited and waited, as the Pacific Great Eastern Railway was built from Squamish north towards Lillooet. Then, though they had no money, they somehow managed to acquire the $600 they needed to buy ten acres (four hectares) of land from the old-timer who owned it. Said old-timer ran through the money in town in no time at all, returned broke and offered the rest of the property at a bargain price. The Philips bought, and Myrtle's father and brothers came west to help build the lodge.

Myrtle fed railway crews as long as they were building the railway. The toot on the railway whistle alerted her that the crews were en route; by the time the train had turned and come back to Alta Lake, breakfast would be ready. Once the rails were in service, the Philips catered to the fishing and tourist trade; in the early years, room, board and fishing cost two dollars a day. Since there were no dining cars on the train to Lillooet, Rainbow Lodge filled in the gap. Each day the train ran, Philip phoned on the emergency wire strung along the tracks to find out how many passengers would arrive. Her meals were famous—meat, trout, wild duck, home-grown vegetables, huckleberry pie, hot biscuits. When snowslides buried a train on its way to Lillooet, a snow plow was dispatched to dig it out, and Philip took in the crew. Several days later, she led them out fifteen miles (twenty-four kilometres) along forest trails, packing the lunchtime hard-boiled eggs on her back.

Philip soon discovered that dresses were not practical in the wilderness. "I used to have to go and do outside work," she told a reporter when she was eighty years old, "cut wood or harness a horse or something, and you can't do that in skirts. You couldn't buy slacks—not like we know them today—so I made my own riding breeks. Later on, I got jeans and cowboy boots."[19]

She nursed when necessary, looked after other people's children, served on the school board for many years (a local school is named for her), and was deeply involved in community activities. She died in 1986, at the age of ninety-five, another of British Columbia's independent women hotel keepers.

Notes:

[1] Cheadle, Walter. *Cheadle's Journal of a Trip Across Canada, 1862-1863* (Edmonton: M.G. Hurtig Ltd., 1971), p. 267.

[2] *Cariboo Sentinel*, June 25, 1866.

[3] as quoted in Wright, Richard Thomas. *Barkerville: Williams Creek, Cariboo, a Gold-Rush Experience* (Williams Lake: Winter Quarters Press, 1998), p. 49.

[4] *Cariboo Sentinel*, July 1, 1867.

[5] *Cariboo Sentinel*, June 15, 1872.

[6] Ibid.

[7] Ibid.

[8] Ibid.

[9] *Vancouver World*, as quoted in Patenaude, Branwen. *Trails to Gold* (Victoria: Horsdal and Schubart, 1995), p. 168.

[10] Cheadle. *Cheadle's Journal of a Trip Across Canada*, p. 253.

[11] *Cariboo Sentinel*, September 10, 1870.

[12] *First History of Rossland* (Rossland: Stunden & Perin, 1897).

[13] Ibid.

[14] McRaye, Walter. *Pauline Johnson and Friends* (Toronto: Ryerson Press, 1947), p. 100.

[15] *Vancouver Sunday Province*, July 24, 1927.

[16] Carr, Emily. "Nootka Had a Hotel," BCA Emily Carr collection, MG 30, D 215, Vol. 11.

[17] Ibid.

[18] Dora Homan collection, Quesnel and District Museum and Archives.

[19] *Vancouver Province*, November 4, 1971.

ANYTHING BUT
ANGELS IN PETTICOATS
Shady Ladies, Stage Ladies

Down the muddy road they swaggered, dressed in men's clothing, cursing anyone who got in their way. In the saloon, they lit up cigars or tucked quids of chewing tobacco into their cheeks as they contemplated their poker hands. "Anything but the angels in petticoats that heaven intended they should be,"[1] huffed a correspondent to the *British Colonist* newspaper in Victoria—but what chance would angels in petticoats have stood in the rough-and-tumble mining town of Barkerville in 1862?

The discovery of gold on the Fraser River in 1857 precipitated a gold rush into British Columbia that transformed the region. Almost overnight, genteel Fort Victoria became Victoria, the seaport, where thousands disembarked on their way to the goldfields. On the mainland, men hurried north on foot, on horseback, in rude contrivances, on rough native and fur-trade trails to seek the mother lode. And where the mother lode was found, deep in Cariboo country, men quickly built shacks and stores, hotels and restaurants and laundries. And, of course, houses for brothels. For, while women did little mining of gold, some were experts at the mining of men.

The newspaper correspondent suggested that there were just two respectable married women on the Cariboo's Williams Creek in 1862, but nine prostitutes. "Each has a revolver or a bowie-knife attached to her waist, and it is quite a common occurrence to see one or more women dressed in male attire playing poker in the saloons, or drinking whiskey at the bars. They are a degraded set, and all good men in the vicinity wish them hundreds of miles away."[2] What the women were counting on, of course, was that there were many not-so-good men in the vicinity. In every town, in every mineral rush in British Columbia from 1858 through the 1930s, prostitutes came to earn their keep, and perhaps to earn a small fortune from a commodity that was in short supply in regions where few women ventured.

"Steamers brought in two prostitutes, white woman & negress, having spent the season in Cariboo (made fortune),"[3] noted Walter Cheadle in October of 1863, as he stopped briefly at Little Lillooet Lake on his way to see the excitement in the Cariboo. This passing reference in the account written by one of the region's best-known diarists suggests that women who were tough and so-inclined could do well in the sex trade. Some prostitutes, of course, particularly Chinese and native women, had little choice: they were sold into prostitution or drawn in by their circumstances or by the men who controlled them. But there were other women for whom prostitution was simply a good way to make a living. A number rose through the ranks to become madams, owning and operating small brothels—though madam was also a

Photographs of prostitutes are rare — except in police files. The four women in these photographs, smiling and well-dressed, were arrested in Victoria in the same week of June, 1909, probably charged in a politically motivated police cleanup. Interestingly, though one was charged with being an inmate of a house of prostitution, the keeper of the house was not arrested. From left, Nellie Anderson, age thirty, was fined twenty dollars; twenty-year-old Mrs. Louis Cutter, AKA Sadie Vernon or Sinclair, was fined twenty-five dollars; nineteen-year-old Beatrice Ferguson was handed over to her mother; and seventeen-year-old Margaret Walker was sent home to New Westminster.
(City of Victoria Police Department Archives)

courtesy title extended to women who owned their own houses and worked on their own.

Though none has written her memoirs, the actions of those who chose this profession and the descriptions of them by men who enjoyed their presence suggest that they were little troubled by society's rules and judgements. For them, the trek to distant mining camps on difficult trails and life in those camps was both an adventure and a business venture. In these frontier mining camps and burgeoning towns, where there were many more men than women, demand for sex exceeded the supply, and there was money to be made in the supply. However well patrolled by the employer, whatever the complaints of the clergy, the same was true in railway construction camps, fish-cannery towns and anywhere single men gathered to work hard and play harder.

Mention of these women in print is rare enough, and almost always sly: they represented a side of life rigorously ignored in pioneer histories. They were "soiled doves" or "sporting girls," "painted and bedizened women" or "women of the unfortunate class." They lived in houses on the outskirts of town, labelled "finishing schools" or "houses of uneasy virtue." Children were warned against speaking to these women, and no respectable man acknowledged them in public—though somehow they always made a living, regardless of how high the proportion of respectable men in town. When it came to writing their memoirs, some of these men fondly remembered the women who lived in the houses down at the end of town, though they almost always declared that it was the other men who frequented the houses.

In Victoria in 1861, the *British Colonist* railed against the houses and against a judge who had dealt leniently with their proprietors: "They are not only public nuisances, but they are destructive to the good order and morals of those who frequent them, and corrupt the minds of the younger members of the community. The Police Magistrate has remarked from the bench that the houses were opened for the amusement of the miners and at their request. We do not believe that any respectable miner, if in possession of his sober senses, would ever dream of setting foot inside of such an establishment. It is a misnomer to call them 'places of amusement'. They are sinks of iniquity and pollution. Prostitution and kindred vices, in all their hideous deformity, and disease in every form, lurk there. The vicious of every class—driven from the public thoroughfares—find there places of refuge in which to pursue their vile practices unmolested, and the greater the blackguard the more certain

This crowded street in Sandon in the late 1890s suggests why madams flourished in mining towns: there is scarcely a woman present in the crowd, an indication of the male/female ratio in most mining towns. (BCA A-03742)

he is of receiving a hearty welcome within their portals."4 To which a somewhat bemused correspondent asked whether it were not better to have such sinks than to have the women soliciting out on the public thoroughfares.

If their names appeared in the newspapers, it was usually as a result of a court case. The madams were competitors who might fight out a battle in court. They aroused the passions of their suitors, who fought among themselves. They got into difficulties with officialdom over alcohol and property rights. In 1860s Barkerville, madam Hattie Lucas threw stones at the house of madam Mary Sheldon. Lucas was described as "a tall and graceful young woman having considerable personal attractions, but unfortunately a passion so uncontrollable that even the gravity of the court could not restrain its outbursts."5 Sheldon, a "buxom, middle-aged woman of matronly appearance, whom the court character- ized as being of sober, steady habits," and who was also known as Slap-Jack Johnny, had come from Victoria to Barkerville to run a brothel.

Respectable men—though probably not respectable women—did have some truck with these less respectable women. Barkerville baker, boarding house owner and pillar of the community Andrew Kelly said he had bought the family piano from Barkerville madam and saloon owner Mary Nathan who, he claimed, had played it with her feet, a remarkable talent and one that led to the destruction of several of the keys.

Also in the 1860s, men who flocked to the mineral rushes in the East Kootenay, on Wild Horse Creek, attended a "finishing school" in Fisherville, where they might take lessons with Axe Handle Bertha, Wildcat Jenny, Gunpowder Sue and Little Lou, who was known to pilfer gold pokes, sing, play poker and even deliver camp-meeting sermons. This passing reference to Little Lou's talents underlines the fact that prostitutes and their houses supplied more than sex. The house was a social centre with far fewer rules and strictures than any other place where nineteenth-century men and women met. In such a house, alcohol was always available, music rang through the rooms and a man could relax downstairs before he made the trip upstairs. Here, a man who was so minded could let loose in the company of women who accepted that men might like to drink, sing and be entertained.

In the 1890s and 1900s, mining excitement switched to the Kootenays as prospectors discovered silver deposits, and mining tunnels were pushed deep into the mountainsides. Not surprisingly, new towns such as Sandon and Beaton attracted many a working woman. Pelle Petersen, writing about his life in Sandon when that isolated mountain mining town was at its peak, recounted stories of some of the women.

"One of the madams there, whose name was Jennie, had once been the sweetheart of my Uncle Hans, who was a bachelor. From all accounts theirs was a stormy affair, and one time, resentful that Jennie had locked herself in the bedroom with another man, my uncle allegedly did fire several shots from a revolver. When the smoke cleared, the suitor came out from his shelter under the bed and jumped out the window, while Jennie, madder than hell, went out to face her boyfriend with the smoking gun. It is said that some of the bullets went through the bedroom door; some went through the ceiling, and my uncle went to court."[6]

Petersen wrote that Jennie borrowed $500 from an old-timer in town when she was building her first house. She invited him to its formal opening, and repaid him before midnight. Not that she got to keep all the money she made: if the flume down the centre of Main Street needed repairs, for example, the town fathers were apt to fine the madams $500. But the money Jennie kept, she invested well. When she was dying in the nearby town of Nelson years later, she asked Hans to come and be with her. He found her surrounded by people he called vultures, all waiting for her to die and the money to come to them. And many a madam was good for a loan to a failing business or a grubstake for a penniless prospector.

One night, an avalanche smashed down from the mountains that enclosed the narrow valley of Sandon, burying the house of one of the madams. The men of the town, led by the minister, rushed to dig her out. "Shortly after there began a heated argument just as to where the Madame's bedroom would be located, and, it was said, there were a surprising number of men in the good minister's flock who asserted their intimate knowledge of, not only the house but her bedroom as well."[7] Useful knowledge indeed: they found the lady under the collapsed oak headboard of her bed.

What happened to the madams when the towns closed down and they grew old? Most left for other places, other professions, but some stayed. Lena Paul ran her business in Sandon's glory days, and was known as one madam who wanted to be part of the community. She came uptown to do her shopping, gave the youngsters she met a stick of gum, and told the boys to behave like gentlemen, the girls like young ladies. When the miners departed, Paul remained, raising chickens and relying on her friends to cut wood for her and playing cards at Tony the Trapper's. In 1929, a man by the name of Joe Harpshaw was arrested for murder and sent to trial in Nelson. It looked like he would get off, though everyone thought he was guilty, because no murder weapon could be found. Lena Paul wanted to testify against him. She told the judge she knew Harpshaw had a gun, because she had seen it in a drawer when Harpshaw came to stay with Paul. "'Well,' the judge said," recalled Sandon resident Lindsay Carter, "'I'm sorry Lena, but according to this record...you've been called up 52 times on a charge of keeping a disorderly house. We can't accept your evidence.'"

Paul was not fazed. "Well, judge," she asked, "won't you let bygones be bygones?"[8] The judge did, but Harpshaw was acquitted.

Prostitution, though tolerated, was not strictly legal, and madams could expect little protection—and some persecution—from the law. Fanny St. Clair lived down past the wharf in Comaplix, a mining camp on the shores of Upper Arrow Lake in the West Kootenay. A busy woman, she was said to serve the neighbouring towns of Beaton Arm and Arrowhead as well, bringing in several girls to help out in summer, when business was especially brisk. Well out of town, her house was accessible but out of sight to those who might be offended by her presence and her activities. The youngster who delivered her paper was too embarrassed to bring it to her door; instead he pinned it to a clothesline, and reeled it to the house. His payment returned by the same route.

That the house was out of sight undoubtedly helped one man. In December of 1910, someone passing by noticed that there had been no footprints in the snow for several days. He decided to investigate. Inside the house, Fanny lay dead. The area newspaper gave scant space to what must have been a sensational and bloody murder: "Fanny St. Clair of Comaplix...was found yesterday morning lying in a pool of blood in her kitchen. She had been brutally murdered by some unknown person.

"Her throat was cut from ear to ear with a carving knife, which was lying on her breast. The room showed evidence of her struggle to defend herself."[9]

Neither the press nor the law showed much desire to follow up on the murder. Rumours were rife—a robbery, a drunken argument, some racial motivation (Fanny's race was never mentioned, though it can be guessed that she was black), some prominent person involved—but the murder was never solved.

Atlin was another mining town that attracted working women. When men flocked to British Columbia's northwest corner around the turn of the century in an offshoot of the Klondike Gold Rush, women soon followed, to set up houses in the picturebook community on the shores of Atlin Lake and in the nearby camp of Discovery. Jenny Bender may have been one of them; it's said that she made her first stake as a madam in Discovery. Later, she worked in Atlin as a barber, then at her own claims on a nearby creek. Each spring, she hauled her gear to the claims with the help of two large dogs, then spent her summers mining underground.

There was no doubt about the profession of Carrie Walker. Walker ran sporting houses in both Atlin and Discovery and didn't hesitate to tangle with both the law and the government if she felt—as she often did—that she was being unfairly treated. Whether her forthrightness outraged the local police, or whether she flouted the law more openly and more noisily than her competitors, she got more than her share of attention. In 1903, for example, she faced charges of carrying concealed weapons, disrupting the peace, and selling liquor without a licence.

Unfair, she declared, and proceeded to write to provincial premier Richard McBride:

> I have a grievance to lay before you—which I know you are in a situation to rectify. I regret very much that I have to trouble you in this manner—but really I can not get any justice here from officials. My complaints are the following, I have been summons & I had to appear in Atlin on charges which I were not guilty—for instance giving Miss Ward liquor—I had to employ atty.-& was at expense of two days in Atlin. Charge was dismissed by judge—yet at the same time Chief of Police Mr. Owens arose in court & said it only means to bring her back or do it all over. My house has been closed ever since & I am prevented from opening the same—as Heals orders are to arrest me when I do open House. Yet all other Sporting Houses are allowed to run & make all the noise they wish.
>
> My House cost me two thousand dollars in Discovery & was the first to build in the lower end of town & then my place was supposed to be the dead line—which since they allowed two other House to go up & run beyond my place & the town. I never kept a noisy place. I can not account for it—except I do not attempt to bribe—which has been reported from some of the others.[10]

Somehow, though not with McBride's intercession, Walker managed to reopen her house, but the police did not let up. In 1905, she was once more charged with selling liquor and once more found not guilty. Several years later, she was in trouble with the law again, this time for bringing in her eighteen-year-old niece from the United States, then throwing her out of the house when she was discovered to have a communicable disease.

Eva Daniels also kept two houses in the Atlin area. "You sure kept might busy some days," she told writer Peter Steele, "especially when you had to take a shift at Halfway," another mining camp near Atlin. Daniels crossed the line to respectable when she married, and took up work as a seamstress. Notes Steele, "She made flannelette kidney warmers, because many miners suffered from sore backs, lumbago, and sciatica. She also sewed moccasin booties for sled dogs. During her later years, she became eccentric and wore a man's hat punched in at the crown and a jacket made of duck and geese breast feathers given to her by an admirer."[11]

In the sky-high West Kootenay mining town of Rossland, the Texas Steer opened on October 12, 1900, and the owners put out a suitably provocative pamphlet to celebrate the occasion. Miss Watson and Miss Harding started their advertisement on the quiet side, announcing a private boarding house for young ladies, but then they were away to the races. "Six Ladies Always in Attendance," they reported. "We have no lady by the name of Millie, but we have Miss Maud who is as hot as To-Mollas…Miners: these are another of our specialties, we were once Minors ourselves. When you are off shift, come down and we will put you on…. We prefer to sell wine, as the Chinaman is small and other corks are hard to pull. We also make a specialty of mixed drinks, provided you buy them fast enough to mix themselves. Ladies and gentlemen addressing each other in the parlor will please say Mr. and Miss So-and-So. To address a person by their given name flavors too much of familiarity, which we try to avoid in the presence of strangers besides it too much resembles a Pink Tea party."[12] And on they continued in this vein, doubtless ensuring that their first winter in Rossland would be a lively one.

Some working women were romanticized by passing journalists. It's hard, for example, to disentangle fact from fiction in the story of Johanna Maguire. It was reported that Maguire was a prostitute in Barkerville in 1862 and that she got lost for a week in the wilderness when she tried to head back south. She survived her wanderings, but somehow in the process the $3,000 she had made in her summer's work disappeared. Pioneer journalist David Higgins wove a much more dramatic account of Maguire—but then, Higgins's work is better known for drama than for truth. He recounted that Maguire first appeared in Yale, the end of navigation on the Fraser and the start of the long haul overland to the Cariboo, in 1858. Then, she was in her early thirties, tall, with blue eyes and black hair, endowed with a strong Irish accent, gentle wit and a formidable temper. Higgins said that Maguire built a shack and became one of the hardest-working women in Yale. Maguire didn't hesitate to curse any man who got out of line, or even to hit him over the head with a chair. But there was mystery in her life, according to Higgins: each week she received a remittance from Ireland, presumably the female version of the well-known remittance man paid to stay away from her noble home and family.

She is said to have fallen in love with a passer-through, and to have returned with him to Victoria, where she briefly led a much reformed life. But the course of true love did not run smooth: her lover beat her, she refused to testify against him and left for San Francisco. How she got back to

Barkerville—or whether in fact she ever left British Columbia—is part of the mystery of Johanna Maguire.

The whores and madams were rebels against all that Victorian morality held dear—at least in any visible if hypocritical sense. Many a travelling entertainer trod a narrow line between respectability and ignominy. In the 1880s, a Madame de la Mothe came to Victoria, possibly to find her fortune, possibly just to survive. No whore or madam, at least if contemporary accounts can be relied upon, she was an adventuress, a woman who relied upon the generosity of men for her living. Antecedents unknown, she apparently arrived in Victoria by ship, fleeing some catastrophe or other in some eastern city. The newspaper reporter who writes of her claims to know all, but delicacy forbids his telling. She set up house with rented furniture; not long after, the furniture was gone, repossessed by the dealer. But she had made at least one conquest. An unnamed gentleman went surety for her at another furniture dealer, and yet another gentleman was kind enough to provide her with a piano. All seemed well, and Madame de la Mothe enchanted her admirers with her performances upon the piano.

But not for long. With no warning, she departed Victoria; noted the *Colonist*, "probably the last scene in the life of Madame de la Mothe, at least as far as this city is concerned, was enacted when that lady went up the gangplank of the steamer *Alaskan* and sailed for…San Francisco."

The reporter was very prepared to give the lady the benefit of the doubt. "Madame arrived here about two years ago…and, owing to her exquisite singing, soon won the hearts of those with whom she became acquainted. Added to this, she possessed a sweet and amiable disposition, and it was seen by even the most skeptical class of people that she was endeavoring to establish herself and make an honest living.

"Many think, several of her creditors included, that her intentions were of the best, and her failure to do well here was owing to her lack of the first knowledge of business principles—economy where necessary....

"However all this may be, her voice will be sadly missed in musical circles here, and her concerts will be long remembered."[13]

Madame de la Mothe was not the only entertainer who came to the west coast to make a living. Singers, dancers and other performers were warmly received in the mining camps, where entertainment was in very short supply and any woman who could be charming and artful—and many who were less skilled—was well received. Perhaps the best-known entertainers in B.C.'s history were the Hurdy Gurdy Girls, dancers who arrived in Barkerville in the early 1860s. These sturdy German women were sent for by one of the mining entrepreneurs on Williams Creek, to attract more custom to the Barkerville saloon he owned. They seem to have been a rather stolid group, and it's questionable how much adventuring was in their souls, but they certainly made a splash in the mining towns of the Cariboo. They worked from nine at night till daylight, charging a dollar a dance and keeping half of that for themselves.

The *Cariboo Sentinel* of September 8, 1866, was somewhat condescending: "They are unsophisticated maidens…, from 'poor but honest' parents and morally speaking, they really are not what they are generally put down for…. The girls receive a few lessons in the terpsichorean art, are put into a kind of uniform, generally consisting of a red waist cotton print skirt, and a half-mourning head-dress resembling somewhat in shape the top-knot of a male turkey, this uniform gives them a quite grotesque appearance. Few of them speak English, but they soon pick up some popular vulgarisms and like so many parrots they use them indiscriminately on all occasions; if you bid one of them good morning, your answer will likely be 'itsh sphlaid out' or 'you bet your life.'"[14] Though the women left no record of their feelings, it sounds as if they more or less enjoyed their jobs and the atmosphere of mining-town Barkerville.

The miners were not as judgemental as the newspaper, and the girls earned well their fifty cents a dance, for these were not the dainty dances of German folklore or the elegant rounds of the ballroom. The miners swept their partners off the floor, competing to see who could get his partner's feet closest to the ceiling. The *Cariboo Sentinel* described the motion: "If you ever saw a ring of bells in motion, you have seen the exact positions these young ladies are put through during the dance, the more muscular the partner, the nearer

Barkerville's Hurdy Gurdy girls look young, stern and a little lost in this photograph from 1860s Barkerville. (BCA G-00817)

the approximation of the ladies' pedal extremities to the ceiling, and the gent who can hoist his 'gal' highest is considered the best dancer; the poor girls as a general thing earn their money very hardly. This class of musician (pardon the misnomer) have also a school of their own in which melody and euphony have no part. Noise is the grand object. The one who can make the most noise on the fiddle, and shout his calls the loudest is…considered the most talented."[15]

All golden dreams die, and the Hurdies didn't stay past the death of the Cariboo gold rush. The *Sentinel* marked their departure: "One of the popular institutions of Barkerville is about to disappear. Sterling's terpsichorean academy will shortly lose its principal attraction by the departure of its lady professors, who contemplate returning to their wonted homes, and these are not in British Columbia. Cariboo toes are not so light and fantastic as they used to be, neither is there quite so many of them. The filthy lucre becomes more precious with its scarcity, and the dance now most appreciated is that which is induced by the monotonous music of the water as it runs over a glittering dump-box. The temples of Apollo and Terpsichore are losing their devotees, who now evince an increasing disposition to frequent those of Mammon. In the meantime, subscriptions for the proposed building of a church are small and few. 'Whither are we drifting?'"[16]

Some of the Hurdies either stayed on in the Cariboo or returned at a later date, marrying miners and leaving their dancing past behind. Jeanette Ceise probably met John Houser in Barkerville in 1867, though the two actually married when both were in San Francisco in the 1870s. Travel writer Lukin Johnston found Mrs. Houser in Barkerville in the late 1920s: "A little farther up the street is…a neatly kept white-and-blue painted-house which is the home of one of the most remarkable characters in all Cariboo. Here lives Mrs. Housser [sic], a hale and hearty old lady of eighty-six, who has not been out of the immediate neighbourhood of Barkerville for fifty-three years.... With her sister Mrs. House [she] shares the distinction of never having seen a train or a streetcar in her life"[17]—somewhat unlikely, since she had been in San Francisco in the 1870s. Jeanette Houser died in 1933, aged ninety-three.

Some entertainers adventured into the deep interior of British Columbia's north, again following the miners' trails to a bustling town or camp where women rarely ventured. Early in 1875, soprano Miss Irving wowed the crowds in Victoria. She sang, said the *Colonist*, "several fine pieces with great brilliancy and effect and was loudly encored."[18] All the talk then was of the gold rush in the Cassiar, far to the north; why, thought Miss Irving, should she not also benefit from the gold? Off she went, by boat and trail, to Laketon in the Cassiar, where miners packed the saloons and might be expected to pay well to hear such a singer. And indeed they did: her concert netted her eighty dollars. Encouraged, she performed again the next night—but once had been enough. The miners stayed away, and the singer returned to more predictable audiences in more sophisticated settings.

Kaslo in 1893 was a booming supply town for the mines of Sandon and vicinity to the west. Hither came eighty dancing girls, to perform at the Comique Theatre, a three-storey building with a saloon on each floor, and a revolving stage for the dancers. Some say the girls did more than dance. The respectable people of the town were sure of that, and ran them out of Kaslo, closing down the Comique.

Florence Wilson came to British Columbia aboard a "bride ship" from England: the *Tynemouth* carried a number of single women to Victoria in 1862. Wilson thought there were better destinies than to become a bride. Despite the fact that the ratio of men to women meant that anyone who wanted to get married could, she stayed single and set up a book and stationery store in Victoria. But adventure beckoned, and she headed for the Cariboo. She brought in a load of books via stagecoach express and started a library; she also ran a small saloon. Still apparently staunchly determined to remain single, she gave herself over to her real love: the stage.

Wilson was one of the founders of the Cariboo Amateur Dramatic Association. That association gave several benefits for her, to supplement her small income as librarian and saloon owner. Said the *Sentinel* on the occasion of the 1872 benefit, "Florence Wilson has been for many years, may we say, the soul of the Dramatic Association, for without the benefit of her assistance in the female parts, it would, we believe, have been almost impossible to keep the corps together.... We feel the case is sufficiently strong to induce all who are fond of good acting, singing and dancing to attend. Come one, come all, and give Florence Wilson the benefit she so well deserves."[19]

Perhaps the best known of the travelling women entertainers who confounded expectations by taking to the stage in the 1890s was Pauline Johnson, who earned her living by declaiming her poetry and prose of Indian legend and the travelling life. Pauline Johnson, born near Brantford Ontario, daughter of an English mother and a Mohawk chief father, was for most of her life something of a rebel and a traveller. Alternating between the self-styled dress of an Indian princess and a European ball gown, she toured at first in large cities. By the early 1900s, she was on the road in small-town British Columbia. With her friend and fellow

Pauline Johnson poses in one of the costumes she wore when she emoted on stages and in halls across southern British Columbia. (BCA A-9684)

recitalist Walter McRaye, she crossed the Kootenays and went by rail and stage through the Cariboo. Greenwood and Phoenix, Beavermouth and Kuskanook, Moyie and Fairview: in every town, people paid a dollar or two to hear her songs and tales. "There was only a handful of people in Camp McKinney," reports McRaye, "but all of them carried into the hall nail kegs and planks for seats, and paid a dollar to sit on them."[20]

In Ashcroft, on the way to the Cariboo, McRaye and Johnson rented a double surrey with horses for $250, including the driver and a change of horses every forty miles (sixty-five kilometres). In Clinton, Johnson posed on a curved stage high above the floor, looking, said McRaye, like a Madonna in a niche. At 80 Mile House, there was a fine crowd with a dance to follow. In Barkerville, they met up with entertainers of a previous generation, presumably Mrs. House and Mrs. Houser: "(There) were two charming old ladies who had been popular in the boom days, dancers in the Theatre Royale in the glorious sixties."[21]

Johnson and McRaye earned $540 the first night, $185 the second, though McRaye lost some of the take when he made the unwise decision of ordering a round or two in the bar. In Lac La Hache, they saw only a few people—but couriers were sent out beating the bushes, and "ranchers, miners, Indians, half-breeds and farmers"[22] showed up in no time. There, Johnson performed in a brocaded silk gown made in London—with the oats still sticking to it, from the night before at Soda Creek, when she had dressed in an oat bin. On her travels, she collected material for sketches she would use in future performances. She also wrote an article on the Cariboo Road for *Saturday Night* magazine, a nicely descriptive poem about Lillooet and other poems and prose.

In 1909, Johnson gave up her touring and travelling life, and settled in Vancouver. She died there of cancer in 1913. Her reputation lived on, as poet and adventurer, one of the women who defied tradition to take up their own careers, whether as shady ladies or ladies on the stage.

Notes:

1 *The Daily British Colonist*, September 10, 1862.

2 Ibid.

3 Cheadle, Walter. *Cheadle's Journal of a Trip Across Canada, 1862-1863* (Edmonton: M.G. Hurtig Ltd., 1971), p. 240.

4 *The Daily British Colonist*, December 20, 1861.

5 as quoted in Wright, Richard Thomas. *Barkerville: Williams Creek, Cariboo, a Gold-Rush Experience* (Williams Lake: Winter Quarters Press, 1998), p. 44.

6 Petersen, Eugene (Pelle). *Window in the Rock* (Fairfield, Wash.: Ye Galleon, 1993), p. 146.

7 Ibid., p. 150.

8 BCA oral history tape, Lindsay Carter, 1976, 1802/3/1.

9 as quoted in Parent, Milton. *Silent Shores and Sunken Ships* (Nakusp: Arrow Lakes Historical Society, 1997), p. 132.

10 Letter from Carrie Walker to Premier Richard McBride, December 21, 1903, as quoted in Steele, Peter. *Atlin's Gold* (Prince George: Caitlin Press, 1995), p. 76.

11 Ibid., pp. 76-7.

12 *Red Book of Rossland: Texas Steer Grand Opening*, n.p., n.d. BCA.

13 as quoted in *The Victoria Colonist*, March 19, 1978.

14 *Cariboo Sentinel*, September 6, 1866.

15 Ibid.

16 *Cariboo Sentinel*, July 14, 1869.

17 Johnston, Lukin. *Beyond the Rockies* (Toronto: J.M. Dent & Sons, 1929), pp. 79-80.

18 *The Daily British Colonist*, March 7, 1875.

19 *Cariboo Sentinel*, October 5, 1872.

20 McRaye, Walter. *Pauline Johnson and Friends* (Toronto: Ryerson Press, 1947), p. 98.

21 Ibid., p. 77.

22 Ibid.

Battling the Victorians

By the time she faced her fiercest battle, Agnes Deans Cameron was a minor legend in Victoria, taking her students to task for their spelling or loutish behaviour, expressing her decided opinions on corporal punishment and riding her bicycle vigorously through mud and over potholed trails. Perhaps this time, though, she might back off from battle with the school board, the ministry of education and a situation where it was unlikely that she could win and where a loss would deprive her of her career.

Retreat was not Agnes Deans Cameron's way: she saw no virtue in compromise. Instead she chose once more to take on the establishment, Victorian in both location and attitude. It was far too late for Cameron to conform to others' expectations.

She was born in 1863, in a booming Victoria that was still invigorated by the gold rush that started in 1858. Though the rush transformed Victoria from a fur traders'

Agnes Deans Cameron in her travelling costume, with some northern touches added, at Fort Smith, near the Alberta–Northwest Territories border. In her diary for her days here, Cameron commented on the native plants, boating and disasters in the region, buffalo, the future of the fur trade, the American white pelican and her conversation with native Chief Pierre Squirrel. (BCA F-08820)

imperial outpost to a prosperous and rapidly expanding town, the sometimes outrageous and unseemly conduct of the miners and many who came with them made life difficult for proper and solid citizens. It was perhaps with a degree of relief that such stalwarts saw the miners depart, life resume its proper pace and people their proper station.

From the 1870s on, Victoria, more than any other place in the Canadian west, embodied the English and Victorian ideals of class structure and proper behaviour. A woman who challenged Victoria could expect a prompt and haughty response. Cameron was born to challenge, as was her more famous Victorian counterpart, Emily Carr.

Cameron was the daughter of Duncan Cameron, a Scot who had followed the lure of gold to California and then to British Columbia, and his Scots wife Jessie, whom he had met in California. One of six children, Agnes quickly gained notice for her sturdy individualism, her quick tongue and her wit. As a girl, she loved to perform for an audience, however small. Though no details survive of her amateur stage appearances, her later life suggests she probably presented dramatic pieces and monologues.

She got her first teaching job when she was eighteen, in a Church of England private school in Victoria. Already something of an adventurer, she went to Comox to teach, then in the early 1880s to the sawmill settlement of Granville, on Burrard Inlet, the nucleus for what in a few years would be Vancouver. There, she established a strict routine for her pupils and a reputation for decisiveness: a sign on the school door declared that irate parents would be received after 3 p.m.

In 1884, her father died in an accident, and she returned home to Victoria, where she taught at boys' and girls' schools, then at high school; eventually she became principal at South Park School, the first female principal in the district. Strong-minded and possessed of very definite opinions about education, she soon made her views known throughout the city. In 1890, teaching at a boys' school, she whipped a boy for misbehaviour. His father complained; the matter went to the school board. In the newspapers, everyone took sides, some declaring a student should be thrashed if he were disobedient, rude or lazy, others saying that pupils should be allowed to rebel.

Cameron had decided opinions on the issue of corporal punishment. "I whipped him severely," she wrote in a letter to the editor, "just as severely as I possibly could. But the father goes further and insists that I struck the boy on the head—this is a mistake. It is within the range of possibility that in throwing up his arms to avoid punishment he may have been 'touched' upon the head; if so it was only a touch and was caused by the boy himself. Every stroke inflicted was a severe one and left a mark. I have spent the last ten years of my life in the schoolroom and no one can truthfully say that during that time, in the schoolroom, I have ever lost control of my temper or addressed a pupil angrily.... Facts, like children, are stubborn things and we must treat with poor human nature as we find it, and not as we wish it to be."[1]

Cameron's absolute certainty about her own behaviour would lead her into further trouble. But the certainty had its good side: many a student in later years paid tribute to her as a teacher, saying they were lucky to have been in the class of someone who cared as passionately as she did about learning. In the tailored suit she always wore, which one pupil later said became her slim, mannish figure, she stood at the front of her classroom, insisting that certain standards must be met. When a pupil won a writing competition with a composition riddled with spelling errors, Cameron offered not congratulations but condemnation for the way in which the girl had embarrassed her school. Interestingly, in later years, the former student had nothing but good to say about Cameron.

Her stubbornness was legendary. In the early 1900s, the city decided to extend Government Street through to the waterfront, an extension that would have run through the Cameron family home. Cameron's mother was ageing and did not want to leave the house she had lived in most of her adult life. Cameron took on the city, and managed to delay the extension until her mother died several years later.

In 1901, she was in trouble again. She and another female principal were accused of contravening a new policy that had substituted written examinations for oral ones; both women were suspended. The other principal apologized and was reinstated. Cameron refused, and only support from the community for her as a teacher won her back her job—at the expense of any good will the school board might have felt towards her.

In 1906, she entered the battle that ended her teaching career. Rules surrounding the taking of exams that allowed pupils entrance into high school were very strict. The drawing examination, for example, must be completed without the use of a straight edge; the required shapes and designs must be drawn freehand. The pupils taking the exam at Cameron's school finished their work and handed it in. Cameron signed, certifying that all the rules had been followed. But, said the examiners, clearly many of these lines had been drawn with a ruler; the students would get no marks for this part of the entrance exam. Students in several other schools were also declared to have cheated.

Cameron refused to let the matter go. She protested to the school board, and then to the minister of education, asserting that her students had not cheated, that she had told the truth and that the marks should be restored. She protested so vigorously that a commissioner undertook an investigation of the incident, interviewing all the children involved and drawing his conclusion: the lines had indeed been ruled. This was not such a heinous crime. The commissioner's report said that a few years earlier, 70 per cent of the books submitted had been considered ruled, and that the following year, there was much evidence of ruling and tracing. Had Cameron been content to be silent, she would probably have escaped with a reprimand, and with her pupils' marks in art dropped down to zero. That, said the commissioner, would not have failed any of her students who would otherwise have passed.

Silence and compromise were foreign words to Cameron. The minister of education said that his interview with Cameron "was not conducive to a peaceable inspection"[2]; a former pupil referred to this as "one of the many situations she seemed to court."[3] She clearly did not know her place. She had battled the school board before, and probably played into their hands now, providing them with a perfect excuse to get rid of her. And so they did: after hearing the commissioner's report, the board suspended her teaching certificate for three years, effectively ending her teaching career. In a pyrrhic revenge, she ran for school board herself, and was elected with the highest number of votes of any candidate.

Her job gone, Cameron had to find a new career. For many years, she had been writing for publication and making speeches. Her writing demonstrated her energy and verve. An article published in *Western Recreation* in 1897, for example, recounted a bicycle trip she took with several others, from Victoria to Sooke to Otter Point, a distance of thirty-five miles (fifty-five kilometres). On a borrowed bicycle, one "grateful and comforting" compared to her own "horse-killer," she cycled through mud, rain and darkness.

Others gave up; one fell when his bicycle had repeated problems. Though they were starving, lunch was not available where they thought it would be. But she was indomitable, returning tired but victorious and describing the trip with vivid humour.

After she lost her job, she left Victoria for Chicago, where she freelanced full time. She took on a two-year job for the government of Canada, to write about the advantages of this new and booming country. Then, in 1908, she embarked with her niece Jessie Brown (AKA The Kid) on an adventuresome trip from Chicago to the mouth of the Mackenzie River on the Arctic Ocean, probably the first non-native women to make such a journey.

From the first words of the book that chronicles her trek, Cameron's enthusiasm, humour, energy and independence are clear. "Isn't it Riley," she wrote, "who says, 'Ef you want something, an' just dead set a-longin' fer it with both eyes wet, and tears won't bring it, why you try sweat?' Well, we had tried sweat and longing for two years, with planning and hoping and saving of nickels, and now we are off!"[4]

In addition to the adventure she craved, Cameron had a mission: she wanted to tell the world, and England in particular, that Canada was not a straight line, length without breadth, as it was so often chronicled by visitors who simply followed the railway west. There was a third dimension to Canada—the north—and Cameron was eager to explore it.

Cameron and Brown set out by rail through Winnipeg to Edmonton, where they found not a single old man or woman in their ten-day visit, for Edmonton was a new and thriving city, with hundreds of people living in tents — though somewhat luxurious tents, with many modern conveniences. By the first of June, they had their kit complete:

tent, tent poles, typewriter, two cameras, two small steamer trunks, a thin mattress with a waterproof bottom and waterproof extension flaps, two blankets and a Hudson's Bay Company suitcase containing tent pegs, a washbasin and a hatchet. Their films were wrapped in oil cloth and packed in biscuit tins; they carried a minimum of personal effects.

And then they were off, on the mail stage that set out into a real gully-washer of a rainstorm, loaded with mail and baggage for every point from Edmonton to the Arctic Ocean. En route, Cameron climbed down from the stage to match strides with a North West Mounted Police officer who regaled her with tales of murder. At Athabasca Landing she took a rod and a chunk of moosemeat, and hauled in a string of seventeen chub and grayling. Then they went aboard their Athabasca transport—the fur brigade heading north to take in supplies and pick up furs, a string of seven "sturgeon heads" or scows, each forty to fifty feet (twelve to fifteen metres) long, with oars twenty feet (six metres) long and a steering sweep oar mounted on an iron pivot on the stern.

"A favourite expression of mine in the latitudes below," reported Cameron, "was 'Oh, I'm glad I'm alive and white.' On this exclamation, I start now, but stop at the word white. North of Athabasca Landing white gives place to a tint more tawny."[5] Cameron slept on board under a tarpaulin, glorying in their progress. "The not knowing what is round the next corner, the old heart-hunger for new places and untrod ways—who would exchange all this for the easy ways of fatted civilization?"[6] Even mosquitoes and rain could not daunt her, though it was a close thing: lying in the stern with their clothes on, their Stetson hats pulled down as nightcaps, and veils over their necks, they could not sleep.

"It is the first serious trial to individual good humour. When each one of your four million pores is an irritation channel of mosquito-virus, it would be a relief to growl at somebody about something."[7]

Her account wasn't just a travelogue of what she saw. Her voluminous knowledge came into play with poetic quotations, the naming of plants, a complaint about the lack of plain speaking in science and educated comments on all she saw.

At Fort McMurray, Cameron and Brown transferred to a steamer for a trip along the Athabasca River and delighted in clean beds and good food in real dishes. Fort Chipewyan, with its old records and native population, fascinated her. They continued on with the Indian treaty party that was visiting every native group to pay them treaty money, sleeping on the deck of a tug that towed a York boat and scow. Where she could, she put out a line to fish. Whitefish was their staple food, though they sampled beaver tail, moose nose, rabbit kidney and caribou tongue.

The Ramparts of the Mackenzie Canyon delighted her; "awed and uplifted our one wish is to be alone; the vision that is ours for one hour of this Arctic night repays the whole summer's travel."[8] But the greatest excitement was reserved for crossing the Arctic Circle; they were now truly in the far north. She praised the Inuit of the north, finding them a most admirable people, and criticized the arrogance of a "white" race that thought itself superior to others. She sampled seal brain, and found it edible—and why not, she asked rhetorically, for this food was no more idiosyncratic than calves' brain and other European delicacies. What's the difference, she asked, between eating the maggots that feed on a reindeer's back and eating shrimp? All the food served here was better, in any case, than the concentrated cooking eggs or desiccated vegetables southerners brought along— though she drew the line at eating muskrat, for she just could not stand the smell.

From the mouth of the Mackenzie on the Arctic Ocean, the duo returned south. Storm-stayed at the entrance to Great Slave Lake, they had some magnificent fishing. Cameron brought in fifteen graylings in an hour on her own rod. "We are the first white women who have penetrated to Fort Rae [on Great Slave Lake] and we afford as much interest to the Indians as they afford to us."[9]

From Fort McMurray, Cameron and Brown set out by boat for the Peace River country, still with an Indian treaty party. At one settlement an illegitimate Cree child was declared ineligible for payment because she had no sponsoring father, and no name. Cameron's offer to give her own name to the child was accepted, and under the name of Agnes Deans Cameron, the child was received into the church, and got her payment. "May she follow pleasant trails," said Cameron of her new "daughter."[10]

Transferring from one boat to another, they continued upriver, feasting on bear meat and cranberries they had been given. Cameron escaped the noise of the engine one day by going to write on a flour-laden scow. Then a moose was seen near the river bank. It had been agreed that she would have a chance to shoot any moose they came upon. The boat crept up on the animal, she fired and the shot grazed its spine. She fired again and killed the young male, about 500 pounds (225 kilograms) in weight. That night, they barbecued moose around the campfire.

Ten thousand miles (16,000 kilometres) Cameron and Brown travelled in their journey. The last short stage in the north was on foot ahead of the wagons that carried their possessions back to Lesser Slave Lake. They returned to Edmonton, then went back home to Chicago.

Cameron's travels and talents set her up to write and lecture about Canada, especially the north and west. She did so in Canada, England and the United States, then came back to Canada to lecture on England. By all accounts, she was an excellent speaker, illustrating her talks with photographs, and speaking with such enthusiasm and eye for detail that her audience travelled with her in spirit. Forty-nine years old in 1912, she seemed set for another two decades of enthusiastic promotion and energetic travel and writing. But she fell ill with appendicitis. After the operation, she contracted pneumonia and died eight days later.

The tributes paid to this "minor national figure" were many. The *Victoria Daily Colonist* thought to be generous in its praise. "She was a woman of remarkable personality," the writer said in a paean several columns long, "in whose case an intellect that was almost masculine in its massive proportions was balanced by a sympathetic and kindly heart."[11] A Toronto paper compounded the irony of that *Colonist* obituary. Agnes Deans Cameron, it said, wrote with virility and vision.

What would Cameron have replied to that? Given her sense of humour and of the ridiculous, she might have laughed. Given how vigorously she railed against the male Victorian establishment, she might well have erupted with the cutting language that she knew how to employ so well.

So much has been written about the artist, the writer and the woman who was Emily Carr that it seems almost redundant to include her here. But she will not be left out: talented, stubborn, determined, eccentric, she was the quintessential female rebel of the west.

Born in 1871, eight years after Cameron, Emily Carr never feared to be thought independent, but never conquered the pain she felt at ridicule. Quick to judge others, she was deeply hurt when others judged her. Though she subscribed to the moral and religious rules of her time, she battled against Victorian—both the era and the city— ideas, prejudices and judgements. A loner by nature and by experience, she distilled her aloneness, her skills and above all her talents into paintings and writing that have long outlived her.

Like Cameron, Emily Carr was one of six children of a pioneer Victoria family of British heritage, who came to the city from California. From an early age, she was the rebel of the family. In trouble at home, in trouble at school for her behaviour, she recounts in her autobiography that she and her younger brother were frequently whipped for their sins. "The most particular sin for which we were whipped was called insubordination,"[12] she recounts, a sin most often committed when Emily refused to kowtow to English-born adults whom she considered lazy and exploitative. As in Cameron's case, her father was the stern Victorian, the dominant figure in the family, and a man whom Carr initially loved, then rebelled against, then came to hate. Carr's mother died when Emily was fourteen, her father when she was almost seventeen. One of her older sisters assumed the role of parent, giving Emily one more authority to rebel against.

"Outsiders saw our life," she recalled, "all smoothed on top by a good deal of mid-Victorian kissing and a palaver of family devotion; the hypocrisy galled me."[13] Throughout her life, Carr would continue to battle the bonds of her family, at the same time as she remained interdependent with them.

From childhood, Carr wanted to be an artist. In pursuit of this dream, she persuaded her sister to let her go to San Francisco to study art when she was just twenty. She returned home three years later, in 1893, then set out again in 1899 for England. Almost from birth, she had been told that England was a superior country, the upper-class English a superior people. She believed it as little in England as she had in Canada. Homesick and often angry at English attitudes, she declared, "I am Canadian. I am not English. I do not want Canada polished out of me,"[14] and rejected all attempts to indoctrinate her with what she called "make-believe gentility." The stress of studying far from home and the distress caused by living in cities helped precipitate a lengthy illness that kept her in a nursing home for more than a year.

She returned home in 1904, adding a few new rebellious acts to her previous ones: she rode astride, not side-saddle, and smoked cigarettes. "Victoria was shocked. My family sighed. Carrs had always conformed; they believed in what always has been continuing always to be. Cross-saddle! Why, everyone disapproved! Too bad, instead of England gentling me into a more English Miss with nice ways I was more *me* than ever, just pure me…. Canadians thought smoking women fast, bad…. my eldest sister gave her ultimatum. 'If smoke you must, go to the barn and smoke with the cow….' So I smoked with the cow. Neither she nor I were heavy smokers but we enjoyed each other's company."[15]

Knowing that she and Victoria could not see eye to eye, she moved to Vancouver, where she opened a studio and painted and taught. Annoyed at what she saw as the frivolousness of her society women students, she criticized their work more severely than they wished and lost her job within a month. The Vancouver years held good and bad: good times with native friends she met across the inlet in North Vancouver, good painting and acceptance of her work, but also loneliness and battles with those who dared criticize her.

She travelled now to France, a year-long sojourn that marked a turning point for her painting. When she returned to Canada, she went back to Vancouver, then made a six-week trip to Indian villages along the coast, reinforcing the respect she felt for native life and the native influence in her work. Her great empathy with native life and history, stemming from her sense of the connectedness between

Emily Carr hugs dogs and monkey in the caravan she trundled to a painting site each summer once her declining health made it difficult for her to travel. The somewhat ramshackle caravan — shown here at Esquimalt Lagoon — cooking arrangements, plethora of pets and idiosyncratic clothing satisfied Carr's determination to be herself regardless of society's comments. (MRS. S.F. MORLEY, PHOTOGRAPHER; BCA D-03844)

the native people and the forest and sea, was yet another rebellion against the wisdom of the times, which suggested that native people needed to be converted to the Christian religion and the white way of life. The only accepted role for a white female in native society was that of missionary, teacher or nurse. To identify with native life and to paint it as magnificent was unheard of.

Later in life, Carr wrote about what these visits demanded: "You have got to go out and wrestle with the elements, with all your senses alert, to see and hear, and feel; there is no luxurious travel and accommodation. You have got to hold your nose against the smell of rotten fish and you've got to have the 'creeps.' You must learn to feel the pride of the Indian in his ancestors, and the pinch of the cold, raw damp of the west coast, and the smell and flavour of the wood smoke, and the sting of it in your eyes, and the awful torment of the mosquitoes, and the closeness of mother earth, and the lonely brooding silence of the vast west."[16]

A meeting with the painters of the Group of Seven in Ontario in 1927 brought major changes, a shift from native themes to paintings that showed even more than her previous works the power and the majesty of the west coast. Time and the development of her art resulted in increased acceptance and praise, but even now, Carr continued to think of herself as an outsider and a rebel, insufficiently accepted by the art establishment. The fact that she could not support herself from sales of her work undoubtedly increased her bitterness.

The Carr sisters, only one of whom married, had seemed well set-up when their father died, but illness, travel and changing circumstances ate into their funds. Art could not support life; Carr tried various ways over the years of trying to make enough money to live on, including breeding dogs and owning a small apartment house. Over time, she became more and more eccentric, ever less concerned with what others might think. Victorians of that era recall a woman who dressed in long, black, shapeless and serviceable clothes that they considered outlandish, but that Carr considered the only clothes that fitted and suited her as she grew increasingly stout. She lived with her dogs, cats, monkey and white rat, most of whom accompanied her when she bought an old caravan and used it as a base for painting sorties around Victoria as ill health prevented her from travelling farther afield.

In the 1930s, she began to write in earnest, crafting the stories of her life, her apartment house, and her visits to native villages with such candour and skill that she was awarded a Governor General's Award for one of her books. As in everything, she did it her way: though she worked hard at her writing, she was loath to accept any criticism that suggested that she might model what she did on any standard and accepted way of writing stories.

In increasingly bad health through the 1930s and early 1940s, Carr died in 1945. Her reputation as a painter has grown over the years. She is considered one of the best artists that the west coast has ever produced, and her work the seminal work in western landscape painting. The image that has perhaps survived the longest is of an independent and rebellious woman, undeterred by custom or criticism, determined to live and work as she chose.

Battling the Victorians

Notes:

1 as quoted in the *Daily Colonist*, June 18, 1950.

2 *Report of P.S. Lampman, Commissioner, re South Park School Drawing Books*, February 23, 1906.

3 McGeer, Ada. "Agnes Deans Cameron: A Memory," November 1974.

4 Cameron, Agnes Deans. *The New North: An Account of a Woman's 1908 Journey through Canada to the Arctic* (Saskatoon: Western Producer Prairie Books, revised edition, 1986), p. 1.

5 Ibid., p. 43.

6 Ibid., p. 42.

7 Ibid., p. 48.

8 Ibid., p. 159.

9 Ibid., p. 242.

10 Ibid., p. 251.

11 *Victoria Daily Colonist*, March 13, 1912.

12 Carr, Emily. *Growing Pains: The Autobiography of Emily Carr* (Toronto: Clarke, Irwin and Company, 1946), p. 13.

13 Ibid, p. 15.

14 Ibid., p. 103.

15 Ibid., p. 203.

16 Supplement to the *McGill News*, June 1929, p. 203.

"WATER!" I GASPED.
"LOTS AND LOTS OF WATER"

An Unusual Job
for a Woman

In a room in Victoria, a slight woman in her thirties sat on a plate placed on the seat of a chair. Each leg of the chair stood on a plate as well, on top of a rubber car mat. A rubber bathing cap covered her head, rubber boots her feet. Yet another rubber mat was wrapped around her chest. A third mat had been placed under the table at which she sat, its legs, too, standing on dinner plates. With such precautions, there could be no "interference" from electrical fields in this experiment.

The witnesses put a map on the table in front of the woman. Without hesitation, she marked one area, then another, then another. To the annoyance of her skeptical audience, each mark correctly designated an area where minerals had been found.

Evelyn Penrose loved to confound skeptics. Beginning as a water diviner who used the conventional forked hazel stick to discover underground sources of water, she soon progressed to using just her hands to lead her to water. As her skills grew, she wrote in her autobiography, she was able to divine the location of oil, gas, precious metals, illness in the human body and criminals—though she chose not to seek the latter, for that would be too dangerous. She divined all over the world, from her birthplace in Cornwall, England, to British Columbia to Australia to South Africa to Jamaica to Chile. For several years in the 1930s, she brought her talents to the Okanagan, the Cariboo and Peace River country as the region's official water diviner. Like other women who chose work as photographers, fishers, lighthouse keepers and airplane pilots, she had, for the times, an unusual job for a woman.

But then, Penrose was an unusual woman; she tells us so herself. Most of what we know about Penrose comes from her writings. According to her own accounts, her life was ever one of drama where she always played the beleaguered but ultimately triumphant heroine. She was the most important—and certainly the most flamboyant—of three diviners employed by the British Columbia government to help deal with the effects of a drought that afflicted the west in the early 1930s.

Evelyn Penrose was born the daughter of a water diviner. Her father had inherited his gift from his mother, who walked about her Cornish town with a divining rod. This shocked the locals, who considered such actions most unladylike. As a young girl, Penrose was in constant disgrace for her tomboyish activities and her refusal to behave as a normal child was expected to. After her father died, her unsympathetic mother dragged her off to continental Europe over her emotional protests. As a teenager, she was expelled from one school for questioning the literal truth of creation, and

In a photograph as self-dramatized as much of her autobiography, Evelyn Penrose demonstrates how she divined gold fields in Canada.

almost expelled from another for flirting with the young gentleman who was intended as a beau for the daughter of the schoolmistress.

Always, through all her torments, she was a diviner. She remembered her father impressing visiting dignitaries with his gift, strolling about the grounds of their manor with a fresh-cut, forked hazel or willow stick. "I have seen the rod skin the bark off itself and sometimes twist itself into a sort of rope in his hands, but nothing in the world stopped it from turning," she wrote. Of her own skills, she noted, "I never had to learn how to divine and I looked on it as a natural thing like riding a pony, and when I was older, finding north with a compass."[1]

After her mother died, presumably when Evelyn was in her early twenties, she went to California to visit the American widow of her uncle. There, she travelled to oil fields and found she had a gift for divining the location of oil. As she walked around one location, she experienced a reaction far more powerful than she had ever felt for water, stronger even than the effect experienced when divining for tin or copper. Jumping, twisting and jerking, she was told that she was near natural gas deposits. Fighting nausea and a headache, she noted that she "still had to learn that oil-divining has a very severe and exhausting effect on the diviner."[2]

She headed for Honolulu on what she thought was a paid contract to find wells for agriculture, only to discover after she had done her work that she had been bilked. Returning to the west coast, she set out north for British Columbia. There, she went almost immediately to the Okanagan Valley, where the main topic of conversation was the drought, then in its seventh year, that was destroying many an orchard. Hearing that she could divine water, several orchardists asked her to a meeting. She told them that she could find water for them, but that it would probably be deep in the ground. Could they, she asked, afford to drill for it?

They could not. She talked to the provincial minister of finance, suggesting that she be hired as the official water diviner for the region and that the government hire a driller to follow her around. Somewhat surprisingly, she was hired as the government's first official water diviner, thus becoming the centre of a controversy, first over whether water divining worked, and second, if it did, whether a woman could be a successful water diviner.

Penrose never had any doubts about her own abilities. One of her visits was to a large and dying orchard. Barely had she begun to speak to the orchardist when she was nearly thrown off her feet by a powerful force. "I grabbed his arm to steady myself. 'Water!' I gasped. 'Lots and lots of water!' He looked at me in amazement, obviously thinking it was impossible that there could be any water in a spot that he knew so well, and over which he walked every day of his life. I followed this powerful underground stream with my divining rod to a little wood by the side of the lane. Here I found the intersection of two underground streams which made the reactions stronger than ever."[3] The water she had found was just six to twelve feet (two to four metres) below the surface of the land, and able to supply 108,000 gallons (almost 500,000 litres) of water a day. After this find, Penrose told her readers modestly, people called her The Divine Lady.

She went on to other farms and orchards. Some men were kind and considerate; others were not. Some made sure she had time to rest; others worked her savagely hard. The head agriculturalist complained to the minister of finance, who had hired Penrose. "She is like a terrier after a rat when she's after water. She never looks where she is going, nor has any idea where she is. She feels or, in some peculiar way 'senses' the water and off she goes, straight into the forest like a shot from a gun. If I take my eyes off her for a minute, she is gone. There are plenty of bears about there too. I'd like to tie a cow-bell round her bloody neck. But, for all that, I've got to admit she does bring home the goods and the people in the valley are crazy about the whole set-up."[4] A note from a less-involved source suggested that she did not exaggerate her achievements. The minister of finance was quoted as saying she had had considerable success, and that the government was well pleased with her work.

Sometimes she was happy with the people she worked for, but on other occasions she had harsh words for them. On one very rainy day, she visited a woman who lived on a far distant farm. The woman spoke rudely, telling Penrose that she was going to build a dairy at one precise location, and that she wanted her water there, and not too deep. "What you want," replied Penrose tartly, "is Moses. He is the only person who could possibly help you."[5]

When she finished her tasks in the Okanagan, she moved northwest to Kamloops and divined at a long list of properties in that region. At one, a cowboy asked her if she could divine for gold. She could try: when an epidemic of chicken pox prevented her from going on to the next town on her list, she went off to the cowboy's Cariboo mining property near Quesnel. Despite heat, mosquitoes and a surprising snowfall, she was more than willing to divine for gold—but she determined that the site had been cursed by "Red Indians," of whom she was very afraid.

Bad things did indeed begin to happen. When she was hiking with a man who knew the area well, they got frighteningly lost "in the terrible forest" where the trees became enemies. An accident happened at the mine; a mine tunnel collapsed. Though everything seemed to have been fine before she arrived, she decided the mishaps were the result of the curse and fled back to Victoria, where she became very ill. A professor of anthropology whom she met somehow relieved her of the curse, though the cure took many weeks, many curious ceremonies and much earnest prayer.

After her recovery, she was summoned to the Peace River block, northeast of the Rockies, to divine for both water and oil. Once more she found herself "cursed" by a native man, but she also came to feel great empathy for the people on one reserve that she visited. "That one race of human beings," she raged, "could compel another to life in a barren waterless area, fit only for rattlesnakes and carrion crows, seems too cruel to be believed. Perhaps the fact that I have seen some of the lovely spots where the Indians lived before the white man came and turned them out…added to my disgust. No wonder the Redskins hated the white man."[6] Though she could locate only one very limited source of water on the reserve, the native women gave her a caribou skin coat to thank her for her efforts.

Missionary Monica Storrs encountered Penrose in the Peace. Penrose was introduced in awed tones as "the Government Waterfinder." "Miss Penrose was another Englishwoman, dressed most beautifully in smart English breeches and riding boots, but in her belt were stuck her hazel rod and various lengths and twists of wire so we knew she meant business and got rather excited,"[7] Storrs wrote.

Storrs overcame her diffidence and asked Penrose to seek out a spring. "I must say it was perfectly thrilling. First she walked vaguely about with her hands outstretched a little, as if blindfold. Then, she suddenly stopped and took one of the wire coils from her belt. She walked in a curiously meandering path and suddenly made straight for the patch of bush directly behind the house. Before reaching it she stopped and called out, 'I must have a man with an axe.' Karl rushed forward and cleared a path for her with such enthusiasm that I thought my poor little bush would soon be all cut down. But at last she came to a little black poplar, commanded him to cut her a path all around it, circled round several times, and made endless strange bowings to it with a long heavy wire, then straightened up and said, 'Exactly under the middle of that tree you will find all the water you need for domestic purposes.'"[8] Penrose said that fifty gallons (225 litres) would gush forth a day, causing Storrs and her friend to laugh like imbeciles at the prospect of so much water. But the key question, as always, was how deep the water lay. It was too deep; with no money for drilling and no one to drill in any case, they could not tap the reservoir.

At the same time, Penrose was developing her ability to find oil fields, divining without stick or wire. "I stand quite still, stretch out my arm and turn my hand so that the palm and finger tips point upwards and act as a radio receiver. I keep my hand gently moving sideways and backwards and forwards, and turn slowly round. When my hand gets into line with the oil, water or mineral, I immediately feel as if I had a little thread coming out of each finger, connecting me with the deposit. This little thread becomes a string and then a rope and, unless I break the contact by running my left hand down over my arms and fingers, my arm will nearly be pulled out of its socket."[9]

Such physical divining was not without its hazards. One day, she wrote, she felt a pull from two different directions, She used one hand to find each field—and could not break either pull. She threw herself to the ground, dug her hands into the dirt and was somehow saved, though thoroughly sick afterwards.

Penrose returned to Victoria that winter and learned that she could divine mineral deposits from maps, without any necessity to travel to the area concerned. Thence came the plan of her friends, who were convinced she must be under the influence of some kind of electrical current. But all the rubber boots and mats and dinner plates in the world could not stop Penrose, and she emerged triumphant.

She left British Columbia and travelled on to France and England for international divining meets, to Rhodesia, Australia, South Africa, Australia, Jamaica and Chile. In Australia, she said, she found people's illnesses by pointing her finger at various places on their bodies. When her pendulum began to swing, she knew she had found the body's troubled spots. The police asked her to help them find criminals, but she declined because that would put her in too much danger.

She finished her career, then wrote her book, which was published in 1958. She ended it with these words: "[I] feel that I can look back over the years of my life and say from the bottom of my heart I thank God that I haven't just existed—I've *really* lived!"[10] thus completing the story of her life as she began it, with italics and exclamation marks.

⁜

Mattie Gunterman was less of a wanderer and not at all a self-dramatizer. The story of her life and the photographs she took in the wilds of the West Kootenay suggest, however, that she too knew how to live, not just exist. In one of these photographs, taken as were many others with a delayed release cable so that she could be part of the fun, she and two friends play the fool on a stove—unlit, one would assume. In another, she and a friend perch high on the rafters of a room, while her husband pokes at them with brooms— an amazing composition that demonstrates a creative light-heartedness married to great energy and forethought. In yet another, she hustles along on snowshoes.

Gunterman was not the only woman to work as a photographer in turn-of-the-century British Columbia. In

An Unusual Job for a Woman

Victoria, Richard Maynard got most of the public notice for his photographs, but Hannah Maynard was at least as good a photographer as her husband, producing inventive images in her studio as he roamed around the province. In Kamloops, Mary Spencer spent the first decade of the century working as a full-time photographer, doing both studio and location work. Perhaps her best-known photographs are those of infamous gunman Bill Miner on his way to and during his trial.

Mattie Gunterman, right, clowns with her sister-in-law and her husband in a setup photograph in the rafters of her house in the Lardeau. The tomfoolery shows her sense of fun and humour, but downplays the work required to make this carefully lit and timed self portrait. (Vancouver Public Library Special Collections, #2271)

But Mattie Gunterman was special, perhaps because of the story of her life, perhaps because of the way in which those photographs were discovered—but most probably because her photographs were such a fine and spirited record of her life and the community in which she lived. Though in some ways her photography was more avocation than career, Gunterman made the most of this unusual job for a woman.

She was born Ida Madeline Warner in the logging and lumbering town of La Crosse, Wisconsin, in 1872, learning something of photography as she grew up from her uncle, who had a studio in La Crosse. When she was seventeen, she travelled west to Seattle, presumably drawn by a desire to see something more of the world than was offered in the American midwest of 1890. In Seattle, she found a job as a hotel maid and met Will Gunterman, a candy maker who was five years older than she was. She married him in 1891; in 1892, the couple had a son, Henry. While Will worked at candy-making, Mattie worked in the kitchen of a hotel owned by her sister-in-law.

The cool damp climate of Seattle, however, was not good for Gunterman. When she developed a lung illness, perhaps tuberculosis, in the late 1890s, doctors told her and her husband that her health depended on her moving to a drier climate. The Gunterman family set out for eastern Washington, looking for a place to live. It was on this trek that Gunterman delved more deeply into what would be her avocation for the rest of her life. For the first time in the 1890s, ordinary people could take pictures on their Kodak cameras. Mattie was enthralled by the art and aimed her box camera at whatever scenes interested or amused her. Her health seemed quickly restored by the different climate and her new outdoor lifestyle. But Seattle was bustling with crowds headed for the Klondike Gold Rush, and the Guntermans went back to help out Will's sister at her hotel.

The return damaged Gunterman's health and made it clear that she must seek a new home. She wrote to friends and family, asking about a place where the family could live and work. Her cousin lived in British Columbia, in the tiny mining town of Thompson's Landing, on the north end of the Arrow Lakes. Prospectors had flocked to this Lardeau region with the discovery of silver and lead ore. The Guntermans, too, decided to go to the Lardeau, deep among the mountains, rivers and lakes of the West Kootenay. The family packed their belongings and set off on their 600-mile (950-kilometre) journey on foot, with their dog Nero and leading their horse Nellie behind them. In Washington they followed the Great Northern Railway line and the rivers east, to the south end of the Okanagan Valley and the Canadian border. There they turned north, for the Dewdney Trail that led towards the Kootenays. Once they reached Trail, they travelled north towards the Arrow Lakes and Thompson's Landing. Gunterman took photographs all along the route. She had outgrown her fixed-focus box camera and now used a 4x5 plate camera that required a more professional approach and produced much better photographs.

The journey put an end to Gunterman's health problems. "Get out and get the good air, and you'll be all right, regardless of what's wrong with you,"[11] she was frequently quoted as saying; it certainly worked for her.

The family, helped by neighbours, went to work clearing land and building a cabin, with a shed out back for Gunterman's darkroom. She might have liked to make photography her profession, but the family needed the money she could bring in from other work. For the next several decades, she cooked in mining and lumbering camps, while her husband worked in the mines and the woods.

Cooking at the region's most successful mine, the Nettie L, Gunterman documented the daily life of the community. Unlike many another mining rush, the Lardeau attracted families, and the activities reflected that fact: hiking, horse-back riding, dances, hunting, masquerades, boating expeditions, bathing parties and theatrical presentations were fine subjects for her pictures. Indoors, she used burning magnesium ribbon to illuminate her shots. A thirty-foot (nine-metre) air-bulb shutter release permitted her to be in her own photographs. She also flung herself into the fun that came after the work. She and her husband were famed as good dancers, and observers suggested that to watch the Guntermans dance the French minuet and Spanish waltz was to understand what dancing was all about.

In 1905, the Guntermans headed south for family visits, photographing the trip, San Francisco and Los Angeles. By the time they returned, though, the mining boom was finished, and jobs were at a premium. Ten years later, the logging and lumbering industry also collapsed. For these and the next decades, the Guntermans found employment wherever they could. Gunterman could always get work as a cook, for her skills were well known. "She could make a pleasant meal out of almost nothing," said one Lardeau resident, fondly remembering. "She was one of the kindest women in the country," said another old-timer. "If she was baking, and it seems she always was, she would always set out a pie or cookies for any passing sourdough."[12] In 1911, Will headed south to Washington State; in 1912, Mattie worked as far north as Tete Jaune Cache, as the builders of the Grand Trunk Pacific Railway moved west. Henry, looking for work in Washington, found love as well. He brought back the marvellously named Petranella Quackenbush as his bride, a marriage that his mother immediately and persistently opposed.

In the summer of 1927, while the Guntermans were away working at a mine, an arsonist—possibly a neighbour who was known to dislike Mattie Gunterman—set their house alight. It burned to the ground, the flames consuming photographic prints, plates and camera. The fire seemed to mark the end not only of her career as a photographer, but also of her photographs. In 1937, Will died at the age of seventy of a heart attack. In 1945, preparing too strenuously for the return of a grandson from the war, Mattie died of a heart attack as well.

But the evidence of her talent did not die. Sixteen years later, Vancouver archivist Ron D'Altroy was searching for historical material in the Lardeau hills. Purely by chance, he encountered Henry Gunterman, who said that somewhere around the place, there were old glass-plate photos that his mother had taken years before. In the loft of the old shed, they found about sixty glass plates, some stuck together with rat urine, some cracked, but most in salvageable condition. Henry also had albums of prints his mother had made, though many of her best photographs were lost forever. D'Altroy took the plates back to Vancouver, where he and others carefully separated and cleaned the glass-plate negatives, thus restoring Mattie Gunterman's legacy.

<hr />

For many decades, the world of the hinterland and the coast was one ruled by logging, mining and fishing. Cutting down trees, hauling up salmon and piloting the boats and later the planes that served this world was largely man's work. Women were employed in the camps to cook and clean, and in the canneries to process fish, but few of them handled the cross-cut saws that toppled giant trees, hauled in the gill nets or worked on the water. Almost every lighthouse keeper who worked the coastal beacons was male, though most had wives who helped and sustained them. And, as the era of transportation by ship changed to one where floatplanes and bush planes nosed into every bay and camp, most of these craft were piloted by men. Yet in each of these areas, a few unusual women took on what was regarded as a man's job.

Sarah Martin, a Kwakwaka'wakw woman who later married chief and famed carver Mungo Martin, was one who braved the ocean to gillnet for salmon. Her first husband an invalid for several years, she needed to support her family and worked during the season at the fish canneries. But she also fished; she is described as working like a man, rowing barefoot and in fisherman's garb in a big skiff to Rivers Inlet. During the day, she worked at the cannery, but in early morning and evening, she threw out her gill net, and earned $600 a month. Added to the sixteen dollars a day she could make as the fastest worker in the cannery, that amount could support her family for much of the year.

Jean Everett, known up and down the coast as Ma, always kept the coffee pot on at the Everetts' home on Rivers Inlet. That home might be anywhere on the inlet, at one of the canneries that no longer exist. From 1916 on, the Everetts spent three years at the old Strathcona cannery, five years at Wadhams, two at the McTavish Cannery, two years at Goose Bay, then a year or so at Schooner Pass and Dawson's Landing. Finally, they built a house at what became known as Everett's Landing. A big supporter of the fishermen's union, wherever she was Everett held open house for the union fishermen and their wives.

She knew what the issues were, for she had been a fisher herself. She fished halibut with her husband, towed in drift logs and sawed them up on the beach, and fished salmon by herself. On one occasion around 1940, she went out at night with her sockeye net, unaware that the regulations had changed, and she could fish only with a coho net. A fisheries officer was on patrol: he caught several fishers using the wrong nets. Five were fined—but Everett escaped. When asked, she had told the officer that she was using a sockeye net. He charged her on the basis of what she said, but did not check. With no concrete evidence, the charge was dismissed. "I made $135 that night," she told an interviewer. "But it wasn't easy money."[13]

When she was eighty she put in long hours feeding and encouraging striking fishermen in Prince Rupert. She died the following year.

The ocean that pounds the west coast of Vancouver Island and the straits and harbours of the Inside Passage from the Canadian border to the Alaska Panhandle hold a million hazards: rocks and shoals and currents that can spell disaster for a passing ship. An intricate network of buoys and lights warns mariners of these hazards. The blazing beacons of this network are the lighthouses whose beams and foghorn blares signal the greatest dangers on the most-used marine routes.

Once, every one of the sixty-some lighthouses along the British Columbia coast was run by a lighthouse keeper whose job it was to maintain the light, set the foghorn going when fog descended and keep a sharp eye out for mariners in trouble. Poorly paid and little supported by the government that hired them, the keepers of the light endured—and yet enjoyed—the isolation imposed by locations far distant from an inhabited shore and weather sometimes so rough that seas broke over their lights. Though many women assisted their husbands, rarely was the job of head lighthouse keeper considered a suitable position for a woman.

Yet several did break through the barrier. Mrs. W.F. Brydon—her first name is not recorded—began as many lighthouse women did, as the wife of a lighthouse keeper. Her first husband, one F. Smith, took her to their first lighthouse at Cape St. James on the southern tip of the Queen Charlotte Islands in 1918, where his ill health loaded much of the work on her shoulders. A supply ship reached Cape St. James just once every six months; they had no radio and no phone. The nearest settlement was a whaling station eighteen miles (twenty-nine kilometres) away. At Cape St. James, Brydon watched and photographed the thousands of sea lions that gathered on the nearby rocks; she made a garden where she planted potatoes and raised chickens and goats, partly for the meat and partly for the company. After three years, the couple was transferred to Addenbroke light, halfway between Vancouver and Prince Rupert, overlooking the dangerous rip tides of FitzHugh Sound. Shortly thereafter, Mr. Smith fell ill and was taken to hospital in Vancouver, where he died. For the next three years, his widow held the post of lightkeeper on the island.

"Time did drag sometimes," she said of her new and solitary position, "but every now and then fishing boats would call in for a visit. I used to fish often...there were many things to take my mind off the solitude and loneliness."[14] Photographs reveal a diminutive though strong-looking woman, feisty enough to row the seven miles (eleven kilometres) across a choppy sea to visit her nearest neighbour. And there were sometimes visitors—some of them unintended. One Christmas, wind and waves heaved a fishing boat with engine trouble onto the rocks of Addenboke. The boat was destroyed, but the fisherman managed to swim ashore and struggle through the underbrush to the lighthouse, where he spent two weeks as a

Lighthouse keeper Mrs. W.F. Brydon began her career at this remote lighthouse on Cape St. James, on the Queen Charlotte Islands. With a supply ship arriving just twice a year, no radio and no phone, Brydon kept busy photographing sea lions and her surroundings and cultivating a garden she created from the unpromising terrain. (BCA H-06864)

guest. On another occasion, a small boat arrived with a Seattle newspaperman, his wife and a baby tucked into a life preserver "cradle," plus a goat that had made the entire trip up the coast with the family, presumably to provide milk for the child. The visitors got fresh water and continued on north, towards Alaska.

Towards the end of her term at Addenbroke, Brydon married Walter Brydon—though no reports indicate how she found a new husband while isolated at a coastal lighthouse; perhaps he was a visiting fisherman. In any case, the couple continued lightkeeping at Addenbroke and then at Lucy Island until they retired to Victoria in 1932. There was a chilling sidelight to Brydon's career: a month after the Brydons left Addenbroke, the lightkeeper who took their place was murdered, one bullet from a high-powered rifle fired from a distance into his head. Though suspicion fell heavily on a local beachcomber, this man disappeared before he could be arrested.

Mrs. Brydon served some three years as head lightkeeper; Mary Ann Croft served thirty years. Daughter of a lightkeeper who was regarded as completely incompetent in his job, married to a man called worthless in every sense of the word, she conquered the prejudice against women in the lighthouse service to become the first female lighthouse keeper on the British Columbia coast. Born in 1865 on Saltspring Island, Croft went with her father to the Discovery Island light when he received a political appointment to the job of keeper in 1886. Discovery Island was a plum position in the service, since it was close to Victoria and much less isolated than most coastal lighthouses. But he quickly proved unworthy, failing to set the foghorn going when it was sorely needed and turning much of his work over to his daughter. In 1902, she was appointed as light-keeper—though she had to pay an assistant keeper who had an engineer's qualifications out of her salary.

"Croft chopped kindling, packed and shoveled coal, hauled water, overhauled and maintained the plant, and shared the twenty-four-hour fog watches….," wrote light-house historian Donald Graham. "When the plant was con-verted to gasoline, then to diesel, she winched fifty-gallon fuel drums ashore, rolled and wrestled them into the storage shed, and pumped up the day tanks by hand. She cleaned the lens, trimmed wicks, painted the tower and dwellings, fed, clothed and educated her daughters for the next thirty years."[15]

In 1914, Croft petitioned her employers for six months' sick leave—granted on the proviso that she pay her substi-tute. That would have been impossible, so she hired a sec-ond assistant for a short time while she recuperated. That action played against her: when her supervisor wanted to upgrade the pay for Discovery's keeper, the commissioner of lights replied that it would not be necessary to have two assistants if the lightkeeper were a man.

In 1919, fifty-four years old and looking for respite, Croft requested a pension. "I think" she wrote, "that after 23 years' service [she took over from her father in 1896 in fact, though not in title] in such employment as the Lighthouse Branch, a person is due for some rest and something to make that rest free from worry for whatever years that may be left. I could make an appeal a mile long about the deso-late situation of the Lighthouse Keeper in bad and stormy weather, but you know the coast.… I hope you will be able to convince those warmly housed gentlemen at Ottawa that when 23 years are taken out of a woman's life in a lighthouse, she is about due for a recognized and guaranteed rest."[16]

Faint hope indeed. For close to forty years, no lighthouse keeper had had a right to any pension at all. She was told she could have six months' pay, and nothing more. Sadly, she recognized that she could not afford to retire: she must work on. In 1932, in failing health, she had no option but to leave the lighthouse service. She was awarded the grand sum of forty-three dollars a month. Despite all her pleas, that sum was not increased.

She came ashore to Victoria and rented a room where she could still see Discovery Light. Two years later, she was awarded the Imperial Service Medal for being one of "those lonely and faithful servants who perform the highly responsible duties of keeping efficiently lighted those beacons which are needed for the safe navigation of ships and the safety of the travelling public."[17] No extra money was involved. In 1935, Mary Ann Croft died at the age of seventy.

⊹══⊹

By the 1930s, women were beginning to make small inroads into preserves formerly reserved for men. Perhaps no group is more indicative of the changes than British Columbia's Flying Seven. In 1936, Tosca Trasolini, Betsy Flaherty, Alma Gilbert, Rolie Moore, Jean Pike, Margaret Fane and Elianne Roberge, pilots all, formed Canada's first women's flying club. The youngest among them eighteen, the oldest over fifty, they came from a variety of backgrounds. Trasolini, for example, was a well-known basketball and softball player, and held the women's discus record for British Columbia.

Vancouver's Flying Seven pose in front of a pre-World War II airplane. From left to right, they are Jean Pike, Tosca Trasolini, Betsy Flaherty, Alma Gilbert, Elianne Roberge, Margaret Fane and Rolie Moore. (CITY OF VANCOUVER ARCHIVES CVA284-1)

The group's aim was to promote flying for Canadian women, partly by performing in acrobatic shows. In the late 1930s, they held a dawn to dusk rally in Vancouver, keeping one of their number in the air at all times. Trasolini kicked off the rally just after dawn and flew for forty-five minutes. Then each pilot took off in turn, repeating until dusk fell. When World War II began, Roberge volunteered for military service but was turned down because policy did not allow women pilots. The group organized a "bomplet" raid over Vancouver, dropping 100,000 pamphlets that asked for "dimes or dollars to buy our boys more planes." The group disbanded after World War II, having helped establish that, in the west, there were many indeed willing to take up an unusual job for a woman.

Notes:

1 Penrose, Evelyn. *Adventure Unlimited: A Water Diviner Travels the World* (London: Neville Spearman, 1958), p. 13.

2 Ibid., p. 48.

3 Ibid., p. 57.

4 Ibid., p. 59.

5 Ibid., p. 63.

6 Ibid., p. 92.

7 Storrs, Monica. *God's Galloping Girl: The Peace River Diaries of Monica Storrs, 1929-1931*, W.L. Morton, ed. (Vancouver: UBC Press, 1979), p. 223.

8 Ibid.

9 Penrose. *Adventure Unlimited*, p. 94.

10 Ibid., p. 208.

11 Robideau, Henri. *Flapjacks and Photographs: A History of Mattie Gunterman* (Vancouver: Polestar, 1995), p. 12.

12 as quoted in Parent, Milton. *Silent Shores and Sunken Ships* (Nakusp: Arrow Lakes Historical Society, 1997), p. 233.

13 *The Fisherman*, May 15, 1964.

14 *Victoria Daily Times*, July 12, 1941.

15 Graham, Donald. *Lights of the Inside Passage* (Madeira Park: Harbour Publishing, 1986), p. 20.

16 Ibid., p. 21.

17 Ibid., p. 22.

THE DEEP TERRIBLENESS
OF A WILDERNESS
Northern Adventure

By the 1920s, much of southern British Columbia's wilderness had been probed, prospected and mapped. Train tracks led from eastern Canada through the Rockies at Banff and Jasper and west to Vancouver and Prince Rupert. By 1930, a daring traveller could even drive from Vancouver through the Fraser Valley and north, though with some difficulty over rough roads, to Prince George or from Victoria to Campbell River, halfway up Vancouver Island. But huge tracts of the region's northern half were still relatively unexplored by non-natives. West of the Rockies, north of the Grand Trunk Pacific Railway, travel was still largely by boat, hoof or foot.

This was beginning to change. The first bush planes were flying high above the landscape of mountain, river and forest and landing on the myriad lakes far distant from road and rail. Homesteaders were crowding into the land along the Grand Trunk and into the Peace River Block, that region of British Columbia east of the Rockies. Yet much of the north remained untouched forest and mountain, still calling the adventurer who wanted to find a wilderness of her own. The women who heeded that call found more ease than Nellie Cashman: with the railway had come growing towns and settlements and help was ever nearer at hand. But the exploits undertaken by the women wooed to the north after World War I are no less compelling than those of the nineteenth century.

The north has always been a region for the unusual woman and the strong one. In the early nineteenth century, Hudson's Bay Company employee Robert Campbell was trekking through the region near the Tuya River, north of Dease Lake, when he met a woman he called the Chieftainness of the Nahannis. He reported that the woman and her aged father were the leaders of this native tribe, actually the Thlagoteena clan of the Tahltan people, and that her husband was a nonentity. "She commands the respect not only of her own people, but of the tribes they had intercourse with," wrote Campbell. "She was a fine looking woman, rather above the middle height and about 35 years old.... She had a pleasing face lit up with fine, intelligent eyes, which, when she was excited, flashed like fire. She was tidy and tasteful in her dress." When a gun, a firebag, a kettle and an axe went missing from the travellers' camp, items essential for their return journey, the woman sent two young natives to retrieve them. "To her kindness and influence we owed much on more than one occasion; in fact, in all probability, we owed our lives to her more than once."[1] When they parted, Campbell gave her his handkerchief and all the nicknacks he had with him; the chieftainness gave him her silver bracelets.

A hundred years later, in 1937, Theodora Stanwell-Fletcher wrote in her diary, "We've travelled by rail as far as we can into northern British Columbia."[2] With her husband, Jack, she was on her way to find a place where they could live in the wilderness and collect specimens of northern flora and fauna.

Stanwell-Fletcher was not amused by the reaction to their trip in the small town of Hazelton, at the confluence of the Skeena and Bulkley rivers. "It is no country for a white woman," was the unanimous comment. "J. is a fool if he thinks he can take one there to live. In vain I protest that I want to live in the wilds as much as J. does."[3]

It was country like this that entranced Theodora Stanwell-Fletcher. Meadow Summit between the Driftwood and Omineca valleys is near the Driftwood Valley where she and her husband lived for several seasons in the 1930s. (BCA I-60979)

Stanwell-Fletcher had sought travel and adventure for most of her young life. Born into a Quaker family in Pennsylvania in 1906, she graduated with a degree in economic geography and English literature in 1929, then journeyed with her father, an amateur naturalist, for a year to Singapore, the Dutch East Indies, New Zealand, Australia and Britain, where the two sought out and studied rare birds. Theodora, better known as Teddy, then went on to complete an MSc and a PhD in biology. During her studies, she spent two summers at Churchill, Manitoba, on the shores of Hudson Bay, studying birds and being introduced to the northern wilderness. The experience so inspired her that some years later, she wrote a novel based on her time in the north.

In this most wild and romantic place, she met the man with whom she could fulfill her dream of living in the wilderness. Jack Stanwell-Fletcher was an English immigrant and adventurer who had worked as a policeman in the Arctic and sub-Arctic, and who now wandered the northern wilds as trapper and outdoorsman. Something of a prototypical man of the wilderness, he had the strength and the skills to live in the wilds and a background and intellect that fired her imagination. One can only guess at the conversations they must have had that sub-Arctic summer, and their growing excitement as they talked about living in the wilderness together. Did Jack suggest northern British Columbia or did she? However they made their decisions, by 1937 they were married and that summer they went west and north.

Late in August, they started off on horseback from Hazelton, led by Ben, their native guide, their supplies carried by two pack horses. Stanwell-Fletcher became ill en route, but the group continued, and she underwent a quick if somewhat painful adaptation to walking and riding over the rough and log-choked land. Five days later, they reached a small native and Hudson's Bay Company settlement on the shore of the north arm of Babine Lake.

Where to from here? The couple sought an idyllic place far from other people, in big mountain country, with good forest that had not been burned over. In Hazelton, someone had suggested the Driftwood Valley, along the Driftwood River north of Takla Lake. At Babine, Dakelh native Dominick West considered the question. "After a long silence," wrote Stanwell-Fletcher, "in which he stood with bent head considering perhaps what he could tell us, or perhaps wondering whether he should tell us anything,"[4] West told them of a lake so pretty that he often travelled out of his way just to look at it. The lake was called Tetana.

It sounded ideal. The Stanwell-Fletchers went on to Takla Landing, on Takla Lake, from where they would begin their final journey overland to Tetana. But they waited in vain for their gear, which was to be moved up the lake to them on a freight scow. Jack began to have doubts about whether they should continue: it was late in the year and they had few supplies with them. But Teddy would not abandon her dream and Jack gave in. "Well, we're going," he said gloomily, "but I think we're fools."[5] They continued up Takla Lake, then rode—or, more precisely, walked, for she had discovered it was easier to walk than to ride over the broken ground that lay between them and their destination—another thirty miles (fifty kilometres) north. Then their guide suddenly turned west across bog and through thick forest. A mile and a half (two kilometres) from the river, Tetana lay before them.

The surroundings did not immediately captivate her. But they had made their choice, and over the next few months she grew to love the lake, the forest and the mountains that lay to east, north and west. Her life in the wilderness became a kind of coming of age. "I'm beginning to believe," she wrote, "that complete independence from other people's ideas and actions is almost the nicest thing in the world. J. says he discovered this in the Arctic long ago."[6] Even the fear that she constantly felt became special to her. "It is stimulating to realize that it is the keenness of my senses and intelligence and no one else's which will keep me safe.

Theodora Stanwell-Fletcher looks out from the tent that served as temporary accommodation for her and her husband as they struggled to build their cabin. Many a female northern adventurer quickly discovered that not all was romantic: doing the laundry and cooking the meals were not simple chores in the wilderness.
(UBC Special Collections, John Stanwell-Fletcher Fonds)

It's a kind of challenge to know that if I relax sight, sound, smell, and instinct I can, in five minutes, lose all sense of direction or, in a second, be sucked down a quagmire, slip on a bank and be carried off in a swift current, come unexpectedly on a dangerous animal, or be helplessly cornered myself—and the chances are that no one else would ever know or be near enough to help."[7] The first time she was completely alone for a day, she saw it as a test of character, a chance to challenge herself against an experience she had wanted all her life.

Throughout her stay, Stanwell-Fletcher knew the tension between the independent and knowledgeable woman she was in her own sphere and the dependent and unskilled person she was in this new sphere. She had advanced scientific degrees and no idea how to skin a bird and prepare that skin as a scientific specimen. She yearned for the wilderness, yet was incapable of living there alone. She was used to being strong, to competing on her own terms, yet the native population whom she met considered her singularly ill-equipped to live here. Perhaps those contradictions are among the reasons why the book Stanwell-Fletcher eventually wrote about her wilderness adventure was so immensely popular: far more of us can imagine adventuring in the wilderness with a strong and competent companion than can contemplate a solitary venture. Yes, we say when she expresses her dread or doubt, that is indeed how we would have felt.

As Jack and his native helpers cut logs, planks and shakes, and built the cabin that would house them through the winter, she struggled to learn to cook bannock and moose, to wash heavy woollen clothing in temperatures that dipped ever lower, and to skin birds and prepare them as zoological specimens, coming to terms with a world where strength and skill determined what was men's, what women's, work, and where each person had to do their share of hard physical labour. "At first I was so fresh from a world where courteous gentlemen rush to relieve ladies of burdens that I was annoyed and rather amazed that none of the men ever offered to fetch water for me. As for men helping to cook or wash dishes as they do on camping trips at home, that would be the height of absurdity…. A woman here performs any job of which she is physically capable, including many of which she may consider herself incapable…. The man's whole time and energy are consumed in performing those deeds which only his strength and skill make possible."[8] But it would be wrong to think that Stanwell-Fletcher kept her peace and meekly set about the tasks set her by her husband. She recorded a number of small tiffs and vigorous discussions, where undoubtedly her strong personality, Quaker background and academic training contributed to her ability to say what she thought and to hold her ground.

The cabin built, the helpers left and the Stanwell-Fletchers settled into a winter routine. The snow fell ever deeper, muffling even those rare noises that had broken the overwhelming quiet of Tetana. Their late arrival had meant that much of the men's time had been spent building the cabin, and little firewood had been cut. The quest for firewood became the centre of their lives, its success an absolute necessity for survival. Jack had been badly injured in a tobogganing accident before they had left the south and was not fully recovered. He discovered he could not continue with the hard physical work of wood cutting and she was not strong enough to cut down the big dead trees they needed. They must find help. On a cold January morning, they set out for a small native settlement. They could not find the trail and were forced to turn back, freezing, hungry and lucky to find their way. In her diary, Stanwell-Fletcher recorded her growing distaste for the nature poets— Wordsworth, Keats, Shelley, Longfellow—whose works she had read since her first college courses. "Now I need someone stronger, more elemental, someone who knows firsthand the deep hardness and terribleness of a wilderness and, because of this, the greater beauty and wonder of it."9

A day later, a native chief and two sons arrived and led them out to the lake and trading post they had failed to reach on their own. They spent several days with the trader, then returned with supplies and with helpers who cut wood and shot moose for them. Through the rest of the winter, they gloried in their isolation, enthralled by the northern lights that danced across the sky, enchanted by the chorus provided by the wolves, and failing, much to her relief, to trap a wolf as a specimen for the museum.

Spring, with its migrating birds, eventually followed winter. In June, Stanwell-Fletcher's mother and father arrived by boat up the Driftwood River. In July, a forest fire threatened their paradise, but rain came just in time to quench the flames. Jack had to leave suddenly, headed for Prince George, impelled by a horrendous abscessed tooth. He returned with a plane load of supplies, underlining how different the advent of bush flying could make living in the wilderness. The parents left and the spawning salmon arrived in the Driftwood River, turning the water to gold, scarlet and green. The Stanwell-Fletchers continued to explore their region on foot, taking advantage of late summer, the only time when the snow receded on the mountains. Autumn and winter came round again, and the couple decided that, for the sake of their family and their work, they must leave by the end of December, when the plane could land on the ice. With somewhat heavy hearts, they flew out—though not without great difficulties—promising that they would return again to Tetana.

Back in Pennsylvania, the couple moved in with Teddy's parents. That spring, Jack returned to Driftwood Valley; that fall, their daughter, Patricia, was born in Pennsylvania. They returned to Tetana in early 1941. This time, their idyll was interrupted by Jack's expectation that he would be called up to fight in World War II, or perhaps by his desire to do so. In the fall of 1941, they left Driftwood Valley again. Jack joined the U.S. Air Force. Teddy stayed in Pennsylvania, working on their scientific report, which appeared in 1943. Two years later, she began work on a book, *Driftwood Valley: A Woman Naturalist in the Northern Wilderness,* based on her journal of life at Tetana. She closed the book, "Keep safe, Tetana, until we come again."[10] They were not to return. After the war, Jack left Teddy and they were divorced. He remarried and went on to other adventures. Teddy remarried twice, her second marriage ending in divorce, her third with the death of her husband.

Driftwood Valley was an immediate success, becoming something of a talisman for both adults and young people in the United States and Canada, who were enchanted by her life in the wilderness and her descriptions of the natural world around her in the Canadian north. The original edition of the book went through twenty-seven printings; it has been reissued three times since, in 1971, 1989, and 1999.

⊹〰⊹

Theodora Stanwell-Fletcher's time in the north was an adventuresome interlude in a life spent mainly elsewhere.

For women such as Olive Fredrickson, their northern adventures lay at the centre of their entire lives. In 1982, actors Ellen Burstyn, Gordon Pinsent and Tom Skerritt brought Fredrickson's life to the screen in the film *Silence of the North*. The movie was a remarkable climax to Fredrickson's remarkable life in northern Alberta, the Northwest Territories and British Columbia.

The tenth of ten children of an abusive father, married for many years to a man for whom life without risk was no life at all, raising three children as a wilderness widow, Fredrickson amassed a wealth of experience that she committed to paper as she grew older, even though she had never been to school, her spelling was phonetic and her grammar was direct. Those stories first appeared in Vanderhoof's newspaper the *Nechako Chronicle*, then in the American magazine *Outdoor Life*, where they occasioned more letters from readers than almost any other article the magazine had ever published. Writer/editor Ben Fast then contracted with Fredrickson to turn the stories into a book that sold more than 100,000 copies, was translated into a number of other languages, was selected as a *Reader's Digest* book of the month and ended up on screen.

Born in Wisconsin in 1901, Fredrickson moved with her parents and siblings to northern Alberta in 1909. Her father had a taste for alcohol and for drunken violence; he inflicted many a whipping and beating on his children. Her mother was an epileptic who died when her daughter was nine years old. Not long after her death, the family made a harrowing and ill-planned move farther north, to a homestead between Edmonton and the Peace River region. Though her life was far from easy, her father still a violent man and her wish to go to school stymied, Fredrickson was not an unhappy child:

she loved the outdoor life, especially when she moved again, this time to live with one of her brothers and his wife. Riding bareback through the hay meadows and the woods, spending musical evenings with her brothers and sisters, driving livestock down to winter pasture and learning to shoot and trap were all part of this life.

So was falling in love. Fredrickson said later that she fell in love when she was twelve, when she first met Walter Reamer, who came with his family to stay at the farm. Then he disappeared from her life, to reappear when she was nineteen and engaged to another man. Walter, her family told her, was fiddle-footed, little better than a bum, a man who would always be on the move and would never provide his wife and family with any security. Headstrong and determined, she would not listen—or she listened and did not care, for adventure was in her nature as well as in his. She broke her engagement and, over her family's strong objections, eloped with Walter.

Her life unfolded as her family had predicted. The couple's first home was a tiny trapper's shack thirty miles (fifty kilometres) north of Athabasca Landing, in fur-trapping country. They lived on moose and deer and bannock,

Olive Fredrickson at thirty-nine: the wilderness adventurer dressed up for this visit to a photo studio, so different from her usual routine of battling the vicissitudes of life in the wild Canadian north.
(PHOTO COURTESY OF OLIVE TORP)

following a trapline behind the dog team that carried their supplies. A few months later, they were on the move: in the first sixteen months of their marriage, they moved four times. "Walter was afflicted with a fatal wanderlust," wrote Fredrickson in her co-authored book. "For him there was always some other place where game and fur were more plentiful, opportunities better."[11]

Their first child was born in 1922, when she was twenty-one. A month after their daughter's birth, the couple took the train to the end of steel near Fort McMurray. Town life didn't last long. Soon they were underway again, this time even farther north where they had heard work was available on a road-building crew. Late that summer, just as they were about to move back to Fort McMurray, Walter heard of good trapping country near Great Slave Lake, in the Northwest Territories. Again, the family set out with traps and supplies, on a scow headed downriver on the Slave. The trappers who had told Walter about the trapping opportunities also told him where to stop and build a cabin for the winter. Once they had the cabin built, they discovered they had settled in on the wrong side of the river, for the fur-bearing animals made their homes on the opposite side. In a clumsy home-made boat, they crossed the river and built a second, ramshackle cabin, planning to return to the good cabin after the river froze and they could no longer trap. The move began a series of bad decisions and led to a miserable winter.

For various reasons, they decided not to move back to their original location as winter progressed. They had left their fishing equipment on the far side of the river, there were no animals they could shoot for meat and, by February, they knew they must move or starve. At forty degrees below zero, their tiny daughter wrapped in their only bedroll, they set out with their half-starved dogs pulling their rickety toboggan, hoping to reach safety at Fort Smith. Hungry and exhausted, they arrived finally at a trappers' cabin forty-six miles (seventy-five kilometres) away. The trip convinced them they could not reach Fort Smith and salvation. Their only choice was to return to their poor cabin and somehow survive on the scant supplies the trappers had been able to spare.

To get closer to a possible food supply, they then moved to the shore of a lake and lived in a tent. As wolves howled around them, they tried to trap muskrats for food, though the lake was still frozen. For want of food to feed them, they shot their dogs. In May, as the weather and their food supply improved, the ammunition in the tent exploded. Almost all that they possessed burned. They struggled back to their cabin, to find a wolverine had eaten the muskrat carcasses they had cached. Waiting for the ice to break up so that they could escape by river, Fredrickson went hunting for muskrat. Her gun blew back in her face; bleeding and half-blind, she groped her way back to the cabin. Her injured eye never fully recovered, and now they knew the gun could not be trusted. "[Walter] vowed that if we got out alive, he was through with the north for good," wrote Olive, "but I doubted that."[12]

For three days, they drank only spruce needle tea and ate nothing. Then the river ice broke up enough for them to venture out onto the water. Six further days of near-starvation brought them downstream to the trappers' cabin, where they stayed for a month until a boat that would take them to Fort Smith arrived. Starvation and near death for herself and her baby convinced Fredrickson that her adventure with the north was over, and she went south to

Washington State and Walter's family. She had been right to doubt that Walter could leave the north for good: he continued to wander and to trap, returning from time to time to his family. Over the next few years, a second daughter and a son were born.

The moderately civilized life she was living in the United States could not satisfy Fredrickson's desire for adventure, nor overcome her love of the wild north. All her life she had struggled, but she still yearned for the wilderness and the challenges that went with it. In 1928, she headed north again, this time to the somewhat more civilized lakes country, north of Vanderhoof in British Columbia's north-central interior. With $500 she had saved from a camp-cook job, she bought a 600-acre (240-hectare) homestead on the Stuart River, forty miles (sixty-five kilometres) from Fort St. James. "I fell in love with it all the first time I saw it,"[13] she later wrote.

She waited for Walter, but he did not arrive. Instead, news came that he had been drowned when his canoe capsized near the Northwest Territories–Alberta border. Fredrickson now faced life as a twenty-seven-year-old widow with three children under the age of eight. She had enough money to build a new log house; in June, she and the family moved in. Not long after, her newly planted vegetable garden not yet yielding food, her money almost gone, she decided she must go moose-hunting. She had never attempted this before, but did not want to ask the neighbours for help, since the hunting season for moose was closed and she wasn't sure what their reaction would be. The account of the moose hunt in the co-written book is smooth and exciting, but the matter-of-fact account she wrote for her local newspaper—where it aroused little interest, for moose-hunting was not an unusual pursuit in that community—is perhaps more telling.

In it, she records loading her three youngsters into a tipsy dugout canoe she had bought from local natives and setting out on the river. "I was afraid of getting caught with meat out of season, so I just pretended to be taking a joyride along the river on a very nice day." Almost immediately, the family saw a cow moose standing in the shallows. "I only had four 30-30 rifle shells and I had to try and get at least two moose with four shells, so I didn't intend to use more than two at the most to get this one, saving the other two until fall for another moose."[14]

She manoeuvred the canoe through the water, trying to keep her excited children silent. Then another moose crashed through the brush, almost dumping the family into the water. They came closer to the cow, but then a small moose calf appeared beside its mother. That was the end of any thought of shooting the cow.

She landed the canoe and carried and led her children to a grassy point, where she hoped moose might be feeding. She caught two fish for an immediate meal and shot a grouse with her .22 rifle. Now convinced that she would not get a moose, she reluctantly began to turn back, but then spotted a young bull standing in the river shallows. She sighted over the children's heads and downed the bull. Dressing the moose, cooking the grouse, sleeping under a small piece of canvas: in the morning the family returned home with a canoe full of moose meat. She canned what they could not eat, enough to sustain them until fall hunting season arrived.

Poverty and hunger continued to plague the family. By February of 1930, they were down to their last few cans of meat and vegetables. Olive set out for Vanderhoof on foot in the snow, following the railway tracks twenty-seven miles (forty-three kilometres) into town. She was out of luck. No merchant would give her credit, though one fed her a good dinner. With no money to pay for a bed, she trekked on in the darkness to another small community nineteen miles (thirty kilometres) farther east. There, the storekeeper, impressed by her odyssey, gave her credit, and she started out again with four pairs of rubber boots for the family and twenty-four pounds (eleven kilograms) of supplies on her back, through newly fallen wet snow. Forcing herself to stay awake, she finally arrived back home, again in darkness.

Life on the homestead improved over time as the garden prospered and the family bought a cow and built up a flock of chickens. Moose-hunting, encounters with bears, the beauty of spring, the smell of summer clover, the colours of autumn, the stillness of winter: she was relatively content. Then she heard that there was a camp-cook job available at the gold-mining town of Germansen Landing to the north. The work there must surely be easier and the pay better than in farming. The family of four headed north on foot, but were delayed when the three children came down with whooping cough. Once they recovered, another nightmare journey followed. When they arrived, they were too late: the job of cook had been filled. She took on instead the job of laundress, work not one whit easier and not much better paid than farming. "When I left the mining camp the following fall I was skinny as a rail and my weight was down to 107, the least I had weighed since that terrible winter back on the Slave."[15]

The job over, she prepared to go back to the homestead. But her children were by now in their teens and the girls especially wanted to go to the city, where there were jobs and young men. In a terrible irony, after surviving the wilderness, her son Louis died of meningitis in Prince George.

Her luck was not all bad. In Prince George, she met John Fredrickson, a big and burly airplane mechanic who loved the outdoors as much as she did. The two were married in 1941 and Olive Fredrickson, barely forty years old, began a new life. Though it wasn't as arduous as her old life had been, it did not lack for adventure. The two spent three years in Port Hardy, on Vancouver Island, but were soon drawn back to the northern wilderness that they loved. They spent the summer of 1946 wandering the lakes and forests of the Omineca River country, prospecting, watching the northern lights, travelling by water and land and having continued adventures, some of them frightening, with grizzly bears. The summer netted them $3,200 worth of gold, more money than she had ever seen before.

The Fredricksons returned to Prince George, where they ran a sawmill they had bought. Tiring of that routine, they returned to a ranch near her old homestead on the Stuart River, where they lived until 1962, when they moved to Vanderhoof. Six years later, Fredrickson's arthritis forced them to move again, this time to Okanagan Falls, in the Okanagan Valley. Her book was published in 1972; in 1981, when she was eighty years old, the film *Silence of the North* appeared on screen.

Olive Fredrickson died in 1988. "She was a very pretty girl when she was young, and she aged gracefully," recalls her daughter, Olive Torp. "Though she was almost totally blind at the last, she was a total uncomplainer. 'I'm happy with what's been given to me,' she used to say. 'I think we've been lucky.'"[16]

The presence of the Misses Pugh, Powell and Lister was first reported in northern Alberta, where they were taking a 300-mile (500-kilometre) excursion from Peace River to Fort Vermillion in Alberta, accompanying the man who delivered the mail along that route. Doctor Mary Percy, herself something of an adventurer in two years of doctoring in this isolated area, glimpsed them in December, 1929. "I was busy washing up," she recounted in a letter home to England, "looked out the window suddenly and beheld three women on skis, attired in the most approved skiing suits etc.! The effect was about as startling as that of three women in Lido pyjamas would be in Ednam Road.... They are known round here as the three mad Englishwomen. It is certainly the most surprising way of spending a holiday that I have ever heard of."[17]

The mail carrier usually took the mail down the Peace River on the winter ice, but that year the river had not frozen over sufficiently. Instead, the carrier planned to follow the pack trail north along the telegraph line, then cutting some thirty miles (fifty kilometres) of trail where none existed. The women were determined to go with him. They left on a Saturday; by Tuesday, the temperature had dropped to forty-five below, with a freezing cold north wind blowing. "You cannot imagine how cold that is," commented Percy. "You *cannot* keep warm by walking, and even when you run and are hot, your face freezes."[18] Blocked by a thick belt of forest, they found they could not continue on the trail, retreated, and tried the river instead. The women survived the "marvellous and exceedingly adventurous trip" quite happily, returning a month later and continuing on across the B.C. border.

Early in February of 1930, the women, two on skis and one on foot, were sighted on Fort St. John's main street in front of the cluster of shacks and houses that formed the downtown of that Peace River frontier town. "They were three English spinsters from West Malvern who are touring North West Canada *on their legs*. They had already wandered about 800 miles in the Peace river country and were now planning to go to Fort Nelson about 300 miles due North of here."[19] There being no road north, they planned to follow the rough trail and were waiting for a team going north that might carry their luggage and help them out at night.

Little more is heard of the three women. We know much more about the woman who encountered them in Fort St. John. Monica Storrs was an Anglican churchwoman who came to the Peace River country in 1929, to provide a religious framework for the settlers in the region, and to start Guide, Scout and other youth groups for the children. Her diaries and letters reveal the country that she saw, and touch on her own compromises between duty and adventure.

She watched the three holidaying Englishwomen as they strode down the street. "I was mad with envy and seized with wild longing to go with them and shake off these suburban surroundings for a little." They invited her to accompany them—but duty called. "[They] couldn't promise to come back here afterwards as they contemplated a far more ambitious dash to the East if it can be accomplished. This knocked me out, as I couldn't come home alone from Fort Nelson or wait about there indefinitely for a trader to come back with. So with deep disgust I tried to make a virtue of necessity and think how much better to stick to my little guns here than yield to a pointless lust for adventure. But I haven't got over that disappointment yet."[20]

That disappointment puts into perspective the story of Monica Storrs. For many in England, her life in Canada was indeed adventuresome, a small rebellion against the expectations imposed on a middle-aged, middle-class Englishwoman in the 1920s. But she looked out from that small adventure to see the much greater possibilities put out of reach by her job, her nature and her era.

Monica Storrs was born in 1888 in London to an Anglican minister and his wife. Bedridden with tuberculosis of the spine from the age of two to twelve, she was nonetheless known as a child with wit and a sense of adventure. Her mother died when Monica was thirty-five; unmarried and still at home, she became her father's hostess for five years until he, too, died. She then went to an Anglican college that trained women to work in dioceses or parishes and to give religious instruction to children. There, she heard a speech by Eva Hasell, an Anglican woman who through the 1920s had developed a system of caravans, run by women including herself, that travelled through the Canadian northwest, providing religious instruction for children and support for female settlers.

At forty-one, self-described as "middle-sized, middle-aged and fatally English," she sought a greater challenge and some adventure. She planned to go to the Peace River country for a year or two. With a trip or two back to England as punctuation, she spent twenty-one years in northeastern British Columbia. For ten of those years, she wrote letters and diaries that described the daily round of her life.

Much of that round involved visiting women isolated in the backwoods, organizing young people into Scout and Guide troupes and generally waving the flags of the Anglican church and British Empire. Storrs was of a type common in England and the colonies: spinsters in middle age, convinced of the values of their church and their country, stout-hearted, at home in the company of women and, as far as can be told, never tempted by the company of men. Biographers have speculated, in fact, that Storrs's friendship with Adeline Harmer, who came from England to join her and with whom she finally retired in England, was more than platonic.

The lust that shines through Storrs's writing, however, is a lust for adventure. Unlike the women she visited at their impoverished homesteads, she was always on the move, walking, riding on horseback, coddling her temperamental

Monica Storrs on horseback in her beloved Peace River country. Storrs sought adventure in the north — and yearned for even greater adventures that lay just beyond her grasp. (FORT ST. JOHN–NORTH PEACE MUSEUM ARCHIVES, 1986.02.33)

automobile, on roads and trails through bush and snow. In her letters, she recorded encounters with horses that bolted, sleighs that overturned, hazardous rivers choked with ice that must be crossed, mudholes that engulfed car and driver, relentless mosquitoes, vicious blizzards, accidents and illnesses. Yet she gloried in it all. In her brown corduroy breeches, moose-hide moccasins, heavy blue or brown sweater and canvas sheepskin-lined coat, she headed out on the worst winter days to visit or lead a Sunday school class. If she could not complete a trip despite her best efforts, she was deeply disappointed.

In August of 1930, for example, she and a companion headed out on a sixty-mile (ninety-six-kilometre) pack trail to visit a woman she described as "the furthest north white woman in the parish." Unable to find the trail, the two women camped for the night by the river. In the night, a moose or bear frightened the horses and they bolted, tearing up their tethers. The women just glimpsed the three horses plunging into the river to swim to the other side, where they disappeared into the forest. Even though they then found the right trail, the women could not continue without horses and were forced, instead, to wait for a man expected to be along within the week. "Oh then I longed to go," she wrote, "you can't think how much. But after a sharp struggle I bowed down as usual to the false god, Common Sense. We simply had to wait and recover the horses somehow…So we said Goodbye to that tantalizing trail—the symbol of everything found too late to be followed."[21]

Storrs was well aware that the women settlers whom she visited had a much harder life than she did. Mired in poverty, often many miles from the nearest neighbour, in a decade when crops frequently failed, winters were long, and money hard to come by, the homesteaders had to raise their children and keep house as best they could, often alone when their men went out to work, sometimes widowed by accident or illness, sometimes losing their children to drowning or disease.

But Storrs treasured the life she lived. She happily pitched in to do whatever hard physical work she could, though she declared that she was hopeless at such things as cooking and mechanical tasks. Sharp-tongued and direct, she was not universally loved, but no one questioned her dedication. She had her own house built near Fort St. John, turning it into a headquarters for herself and the other Anglican women workers. She wrote of riding miles in the frozen night on top of mailbags in a sleigh, because there was no other space for her, dropping off from time to time to warm up by running behind the sleigh. She helped push wagons and cars out of the deep Peace River gumbo. She rode horses and was thrown and climbed back on again.

In 1938, as war seemed imminent, she returned to England. In 1939, she fostered two young refugee boys from Germany, battling the Canadian government to allow her to bring them to Canada. Triumphant, she returned to the Peace in 1940, raising the boys and continuing her mission work. She retired in 1950, returning to England to live in a country cottage with her friend Adeline. She died there in 1967, perhaps still regretting those trails found too late to be followed.

Northern Adventure

Notes:

[1] Campbell, Robert. *Two Journals of Robert Campbell: 1808-1853* (Seattle, Wash.: Limited Edition, n.p., 1958), p. 44.

[2] Stanwell-Fletcher, Theodora. *Driftwood Valley: A Woman Naturalist in the Northern Wilderness* (Corvallis, Ore.: Oregon State University Press, 1999), p. 3.

[3] Ibid., p. 5.

[4] Ibid., p. 14.

[5] Ibid., p. 19.

[6] Ibid., p. 48.

[7] Ibid., p. 30.

[8] Ibid., pp. 23-4.

[9] Ibid., p. 96.

[10] Ibid., p. 320.

[11] Fredrickson, Olive, with Ben East. *Silence of the North* (Toronto: General Publishing, 1972), p. 10.

[12] Ibid., p. 88.

[13] Ibid., p. 162.

[14] *Nechako Chronicle*, July 29, 1965.

[15] Fredrickson. *Silence of the North*, p. 121.

[16] Interview with Olive Torp, June 9, 2000.

[17] Jackson, Dr. Mary Percy. *Suitable for the Wilds: Letters from Northern Alberta, 1929-1931* (Toronto: University of Toronto Press, 1995), pp. 140-1.

[18] Ibid., p. 141.

[19] Storrs, Monica. *God's Galloping Girl: The Peace River Diaries of Monica Storrs, 1929-1931*, W.L. Morton, ed. (Vancouver: UBC Press, 1979), p. 61.

[20] Ibid., p. 61ff.

[21] Storrs, Monica. *Companions of the Peace: Diaries and Letters of Monica Storrs, 1931-1939*, Vera K. Fast, ed. (Toronto: University of Toronto Press, 1999), p. 116.

OBSTREPEROUS, QUARRELSOME AND SOMETIMES UNSCRUPULOUS

Rancher, Hunter, Trapper

Jane McWha Fortune didn't suffer opposition gladly, and it mattered little to her whether her opponent was a lowly native Indian she suspected of stealing potatoes or an arrogant member of parliament. So when M.P. and Kamloops entrepreneur John Mara had the audacity to disagree with Fortune when the two were crossing Kamloops Lake on board a steamer, her response was quick and to the point. She pushed him overboard.

One of the strongest "wild west" images is of cowboys and cattle out on the range. Most ranches were owned and run by men, with their wives helping outdoors and ruling supreme in the house. But some women were equal partners—or more—with their husbands, and a few owned and ran their own ranches.

Though Kamloops rancher Jane McWha Fortune worked in tandem with husband William, she was at least as independent as he was. A "tall, lithe, quick-tongued lassie,"[1]

McWha was born in 1838 and came from Ireland to Victoria with a woman friend in 1862, planning to spend a year in the colony. Instead, she went up-country to stay with her brothers at Lytton. In 1869, she met and married Yorkshireman William Fortune, who had travelled overland to share in the spoils of the Cariboo Gold Rush, then decided there was more potential in the Kamloops area. There, he worked as a wagon driver and Hudson's Bay Company employee, then bought property north of town at Tranquille and set up as a rancher, sawmiller, steamboat builder and orchardist.

By all accounts, the couple were a good match, equally determined and, as Kamloops archivist Elisabeth Duckworth puts it, "unusually obstreperous, quarrelsome and, at times, unscrupulous people."[2] Rumour suggests that William Fortune was illiterate or close to it; Jane McWha Fortune

Jane McWha Fortune and her husband, William, ran a ranch and other businesses near Kamloops, where she quickly developed a reputation for both her temper and her business dealings, which sometimes skirted the law. Jane reverses the usual gender roles here—she's the one standing, perhaps indicating that she would not sit for any man. And the photographer has posed William with a book, although rumour had it that he could neither read nor write. (KAMLOOPS MUSEUM AND ARCHIVES)

quickly became the couple's business manager, signing all the cheques and doing the paperwork as their sawmill prospered and their ranch flourished. She also found the time to pan gold on Tranquille Creek near the ranch, sometimes making several hundred dollars in a week.

She was best known for her tongue, her Irish temper and her willingness to take action against men who were probably twice her strength. On one occasion, a miner from a nearby camp angered her, and she set out to demand at least an apology. The miner was unconcerned—until she arrived. He took one look at her furious face, turned and ran. She followed. He ran faster. Everywhere he went, she went too.

An account written in 1910 described the action:

> At length, utterly spent, and driven to a last desperate move, he plunged into the icy waters of the Thompson River, never dreaming that even a hardy woman like Jane Fortune would dare, or care, to follow, no matter what the cause of her indignation.
>
> But Jane Fortune was as much at home in the water as if she had been a river nymph, and the heat of her anger was so great that she disdained the chill of the northern river. With her first step into the water the man saw his last hope of escape disappear and, without another struggle, he stood trembling until she splashed out to him, and setting her strong fingers into his collar, dragged him to shore.
>
> What she did to him history saith not, the story going no further than that she brought him captive and subdued to land, and that ever after she was respectfully referred to as "Lady Jane."[3]

The 1910 account also detailed how she treated a native worker who she thought had attempted to steal some potatoes. "She fell upon him like a whirlwind, boxing his ears, buffeting him and knocking him about until he was dizzy."[4] When a friend of the worker began to shout at her, she turned on him, hitting him hard over the head with her broom. The two then wisely left the scene. But she didn't concentrate only on those she might feel superior to: no one was too exalted to feel the effects of her wrath, as her act of heaving John Mara overboard demonstrated.

The Fortunes were not strangers to courtroom battles, nor were they considered good neighbours. William was charged with stealing and butchering a neighbour's cattle, and there were arguments over fences. In 1888, the Fortunes sold the Tranquille ranch and moved into town, where they built several business blocks. In 1892, they repossessed Tranquille—including an eighteen-room mansion built by the new owners—when payments were not made, and returned there to live. Jane later sued the city of Kamloops over an easement across their property. Then in 1907, they sold Tranquille for use as a tuberculosis sanatorium. Once more, they were taken to court, this time by a real estate agent who declared he had been promised a commission in the sale. The trial was the talk of the town: William, seemingly a little gaga, expostulated about some roses that the plaintiff had picked without permission; the agent was sparing with the truth; and Jane spoke out in her usual forthright, if perhaps not entirely honest, way. They lost the case, but the sale went through, and they headed off on a six-month cruise around the world.

William Fortune died in 1914 at the age of eighty. The next year, Jane fell and broke her hip. Confined to bed from then on, she died in 1918, leaving behind a legion of colourful stories that made her a local legend.

Like most of the few women who ran ranches by themselves, Kwan Yee was a widow. But she did not take over a ranch when her husband died; she bought a ranch on her own. Lee Yee, born in Victoria in 1861, was just fourteen when she married Kwan Yip, a former placer miner who had sluiced the rivers near Barkerville for gold. After he left the goldfields, he started the Yee Yick general store near Cache Creek; here he brought his new bride in 1875. For twenty-six years, the Kwans ran the store as their family grew to seven children, selling groceries and all the wide variety of goods required of a country store.

In 1901, Kwan Yip died. Kwan Yee continued at the store, exchanging beans and potatoes she grew for goods to sell. Then family friend Joe Duck told her about the Upper Hat Creek area, where he owned a large ranch. Kwan decided that ranch life offered more opportunities. In 1907, she homesteaded high up Hat Creek. Eventually, she joined up with Duck and had two more children with him.

Thelma Mercer came to the Cariboo, near Quesnel, with her family as a child. She married a World War I veteran when she was just sixteen, and the couple claimed a 500-acre (200-hectare) homestead, built a log cabin and acquired a small herd of cattle. As with many other homesteading families, her husband was often away, "working out" or trapping to earn a little extra cash. The knowledge she gained running the ranch on her own proved indispensable after her husband died when their oldest child was just thirteen and she was pregnant with their seventh child. Mercer decided she would not remarry: "I didn't want any other man bossing them around,"[5] she said of her children.

The family would run the homestead and the ranch on their own and with whatever help they could afford to hire.

In winter, she ran a trapline for marten, lynx, fox, weasel, squirrel, muskrat and beaver to supplement the family's income. In summer, she did the ranch work mostly on her own, learning to break horses and brand and castrate cattle and horses. She hunted for moose and whatever other game she could find to provide meat for her family. One winter, her resources dangerously low, she found nothing in her traps—until the last three, where three foxes were held fast. The $200 their pelts brought sustained the family into spring. She also acted briefly as a big game guide for hunters.

Mercer ran her ranch for fourteen years. Then, her youngest child fourteen, she remarried and continued ranching with her new husband for another nineteen years. Interviewed at the age of sixty-six, in 1971, she summed up her attitude, "I wouldn't be afraid to try my hand at anything a man can do."[6]

Ella Frye Creek tumbles down from the Cariboo Mountains southwest of British Columbia's towering Mount Robson in a deeply folded region of small rushing rivers, tangled forest and deep snows. Seventy or a hundred years ago, beaver were plentiful in this region, their fur thick and glossy in the cold winters. Marten, wolverine and wolves also lived above the valley of the North Thompson River along the creeks and ponds and in the snowy mountains. This was fur country, bear country, mountain goat country. As settlers moved into the region after the turn of the century, they hunted for food and trapped for fur that they could sell to supplement the meagre earnings provided by the farms carved out of the bush. Ella Frye Creek is named for a woman who was one of these settlers and who for years was the only registered female trapper in British Columbia.

Frye was one of the few women to run a trapline completely on her own in the west. Though women—especially native women—often helped their husbands, trapping was mainly men's business. Hunting was another story: women hunted, for pleasure, for protection or for food, though few hunted or guided as a business.

Ella Frye's father and grandfather left their North Dakota ranch in 1896, fed up with dust storms and tornadoes, and headed north to Canada, seeking a new place to homestead. On their rovings, they heard of a valley that was west of Jasper in the Rockies, six days' tough riding from where they were and rumoured to be on the route of a railway that would be built in the future. Back home, they loaded their wagons with their family and all their possessions, then worked their way north to Winnipeg by winter, and to the Red Deer area of Alberta by spring. They homesteaded near Red Deer for more than a decade, until the rumoured railway through their fabled valley became fact. In 1910, mother, father, grandfather and five children, plus sundry animals, headed out again and wintered at the end of steel. They arrived at last in the North Thompson Valley in 1911. On the final leg of their journey, Ella's mother, heavily pregnant, had to drive the wagon across a ford on the Fraser River. It must have been a traumatic experience: she gave birth as soon as she reached the other side.

The Fryes were among a handful of settlers at a place called Albreda. Ella Frye didn't start out as a rebel. She and her sisters complained about the hard work of planting and harvesting and looking after the animals. It wasn't, they said, fit work for girls. Their father would have none of it: men and women were just the same and must do the same work. The lesson apparently took. As father and grandfather began working traplines to supplement the family income, Ella began tramping the line with her grandfather. It became her education, for her formal schooling was limited to a few months when she was eleven and another few months when she was sixteen.

When her brother-in-law went down to work on Vancouver Island in 1933, he handed his line over to Ella Frye, now aged twenty-six. From then on, she spent her summers either in the Alberta sunshine or as a logging or construction camp cook, but in the winter, she was a trapper. She built eleven small cabins on her line, at intervals of about seven to ten miles (eleven to sixteen kilometres)— a day's journey on the line. Each fall, she packed her traps and supplies in, at first using horses, then pack dogs, then finally a snowmobile—though she wasn't at all fond of this noisy intrusion on the forest quiet. Day after day each winter, she followed her line on snowshoes she had made herself, checking and resetting traps. Bears were her greatest problem in the early years, smashing windows in the cabins and breaking in to search for food. Charged by a huge grizzly, she stopped him cold with one 30-30 rifle shot to the head, a notoriously difficult shot. She could put up with the bears; people could be another story. Loggers and hunters began to use her cabins as the region became more accessible by road, rail and snowmobile trail. "Where the bears would just knock things around, the humans would take almost everything," she said in 1978.[7]

She had only one really frightening experience in all her wilderness years. On an early spring day in the 1930s, she was on her way home at the end of a long trapping season, packing her sleeping bag, pack, two dozen beaver hides, rifle and axe. Tired and twenty miles (thirty kilometres) from home, she decided to raft down the North Thompson instead of slogging through the underbrush on the river bank. Although stories abounded of people drowning in the river's turbulent waters, she knew her brother-in-law had built rafts and sailed home when he had been trapping. That night, she lashed together logs and branches to build a sturdy craft.

Morning dawned clear and calm. Frye strapped her equipment to a crossbar on the raft, called to her dog to join her and climbed aboard, pushing off into the strong river current. The first hour was bliss: the miles she would have walked so slowly slipped quickly by. The water surface broke into riffles, then choppy waves: rapids lay ahead. "What happened when I hit the rapids almost turned my hair grey," she later recounted. "The raft headed for one big boulder after another…. All I could do was hang on like grim death. The logs of my raft were being jarred loose; one had been knocked off completely."[8]

A second, even rougher, set of rapids lay ahead. The raft hung up on a boulder, rocking from side to side, then shook free and plummeted onwards. Low branches reached out from the riverbank. Frye dropped off the back of the raft into the water and clung to the crossbar. The sweeping branches scratched her face and ripped off her hat. The dog was torn away. Somehow, Frye was able to climb back aboard the raft, now reduced to three logs. She tied a rope to the crossbar, leaped off when the raft hit a logjam, tied what remained of the raft to a tree root and managed to get herself, her gear and her wet beaver pelts ashore, then trekked out to a nearby pole-cutting camp. When she returned later for her gear, her dog came running up, tail wagging bravely.

Tall, muscular, strong and husky, blue-eyed and brown-haired, she dressed like a man and looked like a man when she was in the bush. But, recalls acquaintance Alice Mortenson, she loved a party or a dance; when one came along, she fixed her hair, put on a nice dress, and headed out for the celebrations. "She kept herself up," said Mortenson. "She wasn't averse to makeup, and she would have been happy to use any of our modern methods to look good."[9]

By 1978, seventy-one years old, still sturdy and strong, she planned to give up her trapline. But she had no intention of leaving her Albreda home, though she was now the sole resident of that hamlet. "I have enjoyed life trapping," she proclaimed. "I was never very fond of having a lot of people around me, and as I get older, I find I like them a lot less."[10] Eventually, though, she did leave, moving to Valemount, where she married late in life. She and her husband moved into a seniors' home—she described it as the best trapper's cabin she had ever had, with indoor plumbing, unlike her real trappers' cabins—where the couple kept their door open to welcome visitors. "If there were twenty people in the room," said one acquaintance, "and a child or a dog walked in, she forgot about everyone else right away. Though she never had any children, children loved her."[11] She died in 1995.

Other women have trapped, though they often went unnoticed by the outside world or unregistered by official-dom. Christine Holland, for example, a native woman born at Hagwilget on the Bulkley River, ran a trapline up the Morice River for many years after her husband died on his line, giving it up only when she was in her eighties.

Though some women storekeepers in the north and west bought furs, there were few who acted primarily as fur traders. On her trip to the Arctic Ocean, Agnes Deans Cameron found one who did, at Fort McMurray in northern Alberta. "We call upon Miss Christine Gordon," wrote Cameron, "a young Scottish woman and a free-trader, if you please, in her own right, operating in opposition to the great and only Hudson's Bay Company."[12] Gordon had lived in the Athabasca region for a number of years, buying furs from the native people, with whom she established a firm and friendly relationship. Gordon took Cameron for a walk through a neighbouring native village, where she was handed a baby in a moss bag to inspect, welcomed by a ninety-six-year-old blind chief and asked to doctor a patient with an injured hand. "Visiting the sick, trading fur, cultivating her little garden, bringing wolf pups and bear cubs up by hand, thus this plucky woman passes her days. It takes the adaptability and dour determination of a Scot to fit into this niche."[13] Gordon's one regret, according to Cameron, was that she did not have the medical skill or knowledge that she so much wanted, in order to help the native people she lived among. A river and lake south of the fort were named for Gordon, who came to the region just after the turn of the century and stayed there until her death in the mid-1940s.

Many are the photographs that show women posed with a rifle in one hand and a foot firmly planted on a dead recumbent animal. Most of the hunting stories that involve women recount that they killed a bear that was charging or in some way threatening them on a wilderness excursion.

Women also shot for food: deer, moose and game birds were their most frequent prey. Among the native people of British Columbia lived women who were designated as hunters, though it is difficult to estimate how many there were and where and when they lived since their exploits were rarely recorded. "Their non-traditional job was respected," reads one consideration of several of these women of the Kitimaat nation, "their work taken seriously and the women do not appear to have been treated as anything too unusual."[14]

Several such women were noted in *NaNaKwa*, a missionary journal published in Kitimaat around the turn of the century. "Moodseithlimie is a famous huntress," said the journal. "Her hunting grounds are at Kildala, where she always goes quite alone to hunt bear, seal, mink, marten, and wolverine, with the most surprising valour."[15]

Sarah Legaic was the best known of the huntresses. Her nephew reported that she had a son, but had never married. Independent, she hunted, fished and trapped alone, and only once asked for help—for someone to build a dugout canoe. Shortly after, she built herself another, and presumably better, canoe. Legaic died in 1914 and is buried in Kitimaat. Her tombstone reads, "In memory of Sarah Legaic...the Great Hunter."

The role of gatherer was more customary for native women. Near Lillooet, Shuswap woman Madeline Fox, born probably around 1864, kept the gathering role but rebelled by striking out on her own after her husband and young son died, choosing not to live on the reserve with her in-laws. She moved to a place near Ashcroft, on the Thompson River, which she crossed by canoe, going to Cache Creek to do housework for families living there. But the summers were another matter: then she took her children to the mountains to live in a tent and eat the berries, roots and herbs they gathered according to the old Shuswap traditions. In winter, searching out medicinal roots and herbs, she often dug a hole and curled up inside, covered by branches and bracken.

She remarried, but was widowed again in 1920. She earned her living by going down to the Fraser Valley each year to pick hops and sell the herbs and roots she had gathered to other pickers. A third marriage changed her life little. She still carried her own water from a stream, chopped wood and collected roots, herbs and berries. She died in 1962, almost one hundred years old.

Pilot and airline builder Jim Spilsbury described the relationship his mother Alice had with hunting and fishing. "Dad was never high on killing for sport, fish or fowl," he wrote in his autobiography, "but Mother was a great outdoorsperson and a real huntswoman.... [On one trip] she shot several deer, a bear and a cougar—and not with the help of Indian beaters herding them down the trail. The skins of the bear and the cougar cluttered up our home for many years, draped over the back of chairs. As a kid I hated their smell and was terrified of being left alone in the same room with them."[16]

Alice Spilsbury came to British Columbia from London, England, to spend the summer of 1893 with her brother, who lived near Fort Langley in the Fraser Valley. She stayed on, met Ashton Spilsbury and married him in 1898, when Alice was twenty-seven. The couple went to Lund north of Vancouver for their honeymoon, where they rented a double-ended rowboat, and rowed around the region, spending a week on nearby Savary Island. When Alice got pregnant, Ashton's upper-middle-class family demanded that the Spilsburys return home for the baby's birth. They did so, then couldn't come back to Canada because Ashton got rheumatic fever and was in special care for more than a year. The interval in England changed Alice's life. Since the Spilsbury family perceived Alice to be socially beneath them, they treated her with disdain, little better than a servant. "This sort of treatment would have been hard for anyone to take, but for my mother it was much, much worse. Whether it was her French blood or what, she reacted very violently, being very fiery and proud in her right. She came away from this spell in England just searing with rage. It stayed burning inside her, and the form it apparently took was to turn her against everything that

Alice Spilsbury hunted, fished and behaved as much like a man as she could; attired in her trademark trousers, she was once thrown out of a women's restaurant in a Vancouver club. Here, she's shown on a beach near her long-time Savary Island home.
(UBC SPECIAL COLLECTIONS, A.J. SPILSBURY FONDS)

people like my father and his family stood for."[17] Spilsbury cut her hair short, wore men's trousers, became a suffragette and adopted the cause of the anti-British terrorists in Ireland.

Some time after they returned from England, the family had financial reverses and moved to Savary Island. There they moved into a cabin owned by friends, then into a tent they set up on an unused right of way, squatting until they could afford to buy land. The tent, said son Jim, was actually two tents with a space between and a fly covering all, with a platform of planks picked up on the beach and driftwood covering the front and back. "It ended up the tent was more like wallpaper; we built around it."[18] Alice Spilsbury loved it. When the Spilsburys could finally afford to build a house, she lived inside for less than a year before she moved out. "After all those years of living in the tent, she couldn't stand living in a real house. She would cook our meals when we were working and then she wouldn't eat with us. She would sit there and smoke a cigarette and put her feet up on the table and watch us eat. She lived in a shed out back."[19]

Spilsbury loved to hunt and fish, though she had strict rules on how hunting should be conducted. She declared that high-powered sporting rifles should be banned. She used a shotgun, with different size shot for ducks, geese or deer. "Her method was to walk over the ground carefully, identify the trails, and then post herself quietly behind a tree and wait patiently until the right deer came along, and when he did, believe me he was dead."[20]

According to her son, Spilsbury went out of her way to be different—though a son's view may not be entirely accurate and her actions may have been more innate than deliberate. She wore her hair short; she wore pants, or sometimes knickers with puttees or high leather boots. She went to the Jericho Tennis Club in Vancouver with a friend and got herself thrown out of the ladies' washroom, because the other women thought she was a man. "She regarded herself as a man. She hated women. She used the word *females* in a way just dripping with disdain that meant the lowest of the low. Everybody we knew admired the hell out of her, but I hated to be around her. I would get so embarrassed."[21]

Alice Spilsbury stayed independent right up to the end. In the 1940s, she left Savary and moved to North Vancouver, where she bought a trailer that she parked on property near the waterfront. When Ashton Spilsbury also moved to North Vancouver and bought a house there, she moved the trailer, which she shared with a menagerie of budgies and canaries, to the back of his lot. She died in the mid-1950s.

Notes:
[1] "Lady Jane of Kamloops," originally printed in *Woman's National Daily*, St. Louis, Mo., in 1910, reprinted in the *Kamloops Sentinel*, December 14, 1934.
[2] Duckworth, Elisabeth. "Tranquille Sanatorium," Kamloops Museum and Archives paper, July 24, 1990.
[3] "Lady Jane of Kamloops."
[4] Ibid.
[5] *Vancouver Sun*, August 12, 1971.
[6] Ibid.
[7] *Forestalk*, Winter, 1978.
[8] Ibid.
[9] Interview with Alice Mortenson, May 18, 2000.
[10] *Forestalk*.
[11] Interview, anonymous, May 15, 2000.
[12] Cameron, Agnes Deans. *The New North: An Account of a Woman's 1908 Journey through Canada to the Arctic* (Saskatoon: Western Producer Prairie Books, revised edition, 1986), p. 65.

[13] Ibid.

[14] *Northern Sentinel*, September 25, 1980.

[15] *NaNaKwa*, July, 1902, as quoted in the *Northern Sentinel*, September 25, 1980.

[16] Spilsbury, Jim, and White, Howard. *Spilsbury's Coast* (Madeira Park: Harbour Publishing, 1987), p. 9.

[17] Ibid., pp. 10-11.

[18] Ibid., p. 17.

[19] Ibid., p. 70.

[20] Ibid., p. 22.

[21] Ibid., p. 31.

I THOUGHT I'D
CONQUERED THE WORLD

Scaling Mountains, Sailing Seas

As the mountain climbers edged across the cliff above a vast glacier, rocks volleyed down the exposed slope. One smashed into the boulder that anchored the climbing rope; another tumbled scant inches from Phyllis Munday, brushing her hair. The instinct was to jump back behind protection—but that would leave Munday's husband, Don, without support. She threw up her arm to deflect another rock that could have smashed into her sister, who was behind her on the slope; it badly bruised her arm. Yet another rock hit her head, and blood welled from the wound.

Later, Phyllis Munday described the next moments on the mountain. "They were just fingerholds, actually—just cracks and not much more for your boots. A rock came from somewhere above and managed to use my head for a target. For a minute, I thought I was going to black out. All of a sudden, luckily, it struck me: if I fall, I'll pull Don off; I can't fall. It's amazing. I didn't fall. I just hung on with these four little fingers on each hand until I'd sort of got the dizziness over. We had to come down, of course, because blood was beginning to ooze all over the place. We got down further and there was a sloping rock with a great big lovely puddle of water in it, and I could lie there, and my sister sloshed off the blood."[1]

Soaked by snow and ice, at the mercy of a chilling wind, the trio went on into the dusk, ever tantalized by the spearing peak of Mystery Mountain, high above them in the Coast Mountains. Phyllis Munday was not deterred by the rock fall, her injury or the conditions. "Phyl insisted on taking her share of leadership amid the worst of the naked crevasses" her husband wrote in his book on their mountaineering life. "She sank through a few times, but without other incident we approached the marginal maze. Mastering this, we climbed to our bivouac at 3.45 a.m., twenty-seven hours since leaving it.... Though complete rest is now thought the safe way to treat head injuries, Phyllis showed little ill effects."[2]

Phyllis Munday climbed her first mountain when she was sixteen years old, her last when she was in her sixties. She took her last walk in the hills when she was eighty-eight, despite almost incapacitating arthritis. That same year, 1982, she flew by helicopter to the Homathko Icefield to see up close up for one last time her Mystery Mountain— the imposing peak she and her husband had first espied when looking across the Strait of Georgia from Vancouver Island almost sixty years earlier. Between her first climb and her last, she built a reputation as one of British Columbia's premier mountain climbers of either gender. She and her husband formed one of the most formidable climbing teams in the world.

Phyllis Munday was not the only woman to discover the challenge of mountain climbing. The 1909 edition of the *Canadian Alpine Journal* recorded some of the earliest climbs made by women, in the Alps between 1809 and 1870, and pointed out that a woman had recently climbed Peru's Mount Huascaran, another had made first ascents of peaks on the Himalayas and a third had made at least 200 ascents. "Now that alpine clubs exist which admit women to membership, and which, by assuming all responsibility of equipment at a reasonable rate, place the mountain summits within reach of all, there is no reason why every woman may not seriously ask herself 'Why should I not spend this year in the mountains?'"[3] But the mountain summits that Munday sought were not within the reach of all, and the way in

Phyllis Munday was one of British Columbia's best-known and most-accomplished mountaineers, never loathe to assume her share of responsibility or carry a heavy pack. Here, she stands high in her beloved coast mountains, not far from Mount Waddington, which the Mundays throughly explored, and Mount Munday, named for the climbing couple. (BCA H-3440)

which she climbed them set her apart from the recreational climber. The Mundays rarely used professional guides on their climbs. She asked no favours when she climbed: not for her the safe position on the rope, or the guide or fellow climber who carried most of the heavy equipment and supplies. She took on as much of the responsibility as anyone else, and demanded, received and deserved independence and equality. She would never have said, as one woman did on a climbing trip in the Rockies, that she had always been a coward and never again wanted to be on the end of the climbing rope rather than secured between two male companions.[4]

Munday could probably not recall a time when she was not outdoors and adventuring. Born in 1894 in Ceylon (Sri Lanka) the daughter of a tea planter and his wife, she was taken when very young to England, then to Canada. The family settled first in Manitoba, then moved to Nelson, in British Columbia's West Kootenay, a region of forest and mountain peaks flashed white with glaciers. With her .22 rifle and an old horse named Titus, Munday spent many hours riding or hiking the bush and riverbanks of her new home. The family then moved to Vancouver, and her eyes turned towards the North Shore Mountains that lay across Burrard Inlet. Again and again, she took the streetcar to the end of the line below the mountains, then hiked and scrambled up the slopes. "Going up Grouse Mountain," she later said, "I thought I'd conquered the world."[5]

She climbed the 5,400-foot (1646-metre) Lions with a mountaineering club when she was about sixteen and immediately wanted more. At the age of twenty-four, she met Don Munday, a soldier who had been wounded in the war and a fervent mountaineer. Climbs together confirmed their attraction; they were married in 1920. After the wedding, they horrified their parents by skipping the reception, changing to knickers and boots and heading up Grouse Mountain. For the next few years, they lived in a cabin they built on the mountain. They were among the first to ski the North Shore Mountains and introduced their baby daughter, born in 1921, to trekking and climbing almost as soon as she could hold her head upright. They climbed in the southern ranges of the Coast Mountains in these years, making first ascents of several peaks. But Munday's triumph of the 1920s was on Mount Robson, the highest in the Canadian Rockies.

In 1924, members of the Canadian Alpine club prepared to ascend this 12,972-foot (3954-metre) mountain, first climbed in 1913. Though women were generally regarded as not strong enough for such a climb, Munday and another woman were chosen as part of the dozen-member assault group. As they prepared for the climb, one of the men lightened the other woman's pack by removing some of the items in it and putting them in his pack. Munday jealously guarded her own pack: she wanted no favours, no hint of inequality.

The group crested the main ridge of Mount Robson. "The slope above," wrote Munday, "is unlike anything elsewhere in the Rockies—an absolute chaos of ice blocks on a slope of not less than 45 degrees; domed with snow and bristling with gleaming icicles, they were a never-to-be-forgotten sight, fairylike perhaps, but sinister, hostile, menacing. Even in the bright sunlight, we shivered if we stopped."[6] Late in the afternoon, the group's guide, Conrad Kain, surmounted the last short section. Munday followed him to the summit and was proclaimed the first woman on top of Mount Robson.

Climbers had been tackling the Rocky Mountains since the Canadian Pacific Railway tracks had been laid through the mountains in the 1880s. The building of the Grand Trunk Pacific through a pass near Jasper had attracted many climbers to the region around Mount Robson since 1910. But no railway ran through the ramparts of the Coast Mountains north of the Fraser Valley. The row of peaks that looked across to the Vancouver Island Mountains was difficult of access and all but unexplored. By the 1920s, no one had yet mapped or measured them in detail.

Late on a summer's day in 1925, Phyllis and Don Munday stood near timberline on Vancouver Island's Mount Arrowsmith, looking out across Georgia Strait towards the mountains of the mainland coast. Spearing above the others was one majestic peak, which they named Mystery Mountain. From the time they first caught sight of its glimmer in the evening sunshine, the Mundays were determined to explore it. Some years later, it was named Mount Waddington; at 13,176 feet (4016 metres), it is the highest mountain entirely in British Columbia.

Steamships still ran up the British Columbia coast in those days, calling at fish canneries, floating logging camps and isolated homesteads. But no roads and very few trails led inland along the steep slopes that rose above the deep fjords or through the valleys that cut between the mountains. The Mundays could reach a starting point by steamer or by using their own boat. From the bays or coves where they disembarked, they must pack in their equipment and supplies in painful relays from the shore.

Over twelve years, eleven trips and fifteen months on the ground, they climbed, explored, reconnoitered and sought the summit of Mount Waddington, ever to them

Mystery Mountain. Though they came within sixty feet (eighteen metres) of that summit, the difficulties of supply, glaciers, rocks and weather kept them from their goal. What others might have regarded as failure was no such thing to the Mundays. Phyllis Munday was never a trophy climber. For her, the journey was everything. In her later years, she expressed her dismay at those who rushed in, "bagged a peak" and rushed out again. Asked why she and her husband continued to return to Waddington year after year, even though they never succeeded in climbing the main peak, she answered, "We didn't go into the Waddington country just to climb one mountain and run out and leave it. We went into the Waddington country to find out all we possibly could about glaciers and mountains and animals and nature and everything about that particular area—completely unknown before we went into it—so that we could bring out the information for the interest of other people as well as ourselves."[7]

Climbing was pure joy for Munday. Shouldering a sixty-six pound (thirty-kilogram) pack over rock and ice, through crevasses and into the teeth of fierce mountain storms; camping in cold and dark; chopping steps through an icefield; photographing alpine flowers; collecting insects that somehow survived in the most remote mountain regions: all these were part of her pleasure. Potential tragedies and actual injuries such as that suffered in the rock fall or the snowblindness that afflicted her for several days on one climb, forcing her to follow docilely until her vision returned, were no deterrent. As soon as their daughter, Edith, was old enough, the Mundays took her along on their climbs and she, too, developed a love of this strenuous avocation.

Stories of Munday's strength and leadership abound. Don Munday related how, early in their friendship, rocks gave way beneath him on a climb, and he seemed fated to tumble towards a glacier far below. Phyllis immediately jumped to catch him. The rocks she jumped to crumbled as well, but between them, they were able to find new footing and avoid a fatal fall. On another occasion, Phyllis Munday stood, ice axe at the ready, between her husband who had slipped and fallen and an approaching grizzly sow and cubs. She aroused tremendous respect among her climbing partners, for she was as willing as any man to shoulder the heavy packs, take her turn as leader on the rope, cut steps or test traverses. Said one companion, "I recall picking up her pack once and being very glad she was carrying it and not me."[8] Said another, "Who else but Phyllis would cheerfully observe half a ton of supplies to be backpacked through eight miles of trackless coast rain forest, and twenty-eight miles of Franklin Glacier?...Phyl was at her best when the going was tough and dangerous."[9]

In 1949, the Mundays made their last climb together, of Mount Freshfield in the Rockies. Later that year, Don Munday fell ill. He died six months later, at the age of sixty. Phyllis took his ashes aloft by chartered plane, to scatter them over Mount Munday, a coastal peak near Mount Waddington that had been named for the couple. She continued climbing after her husband's death, though without her longtime climbing partner and in pain from ever-worsening arthritis, she now tackled only the easier peaks.

The love for the mountains never died. "Oh, I would give anything to go [back to Mount Waddington]...." she told magazine writer Bryan McGill in 1982. "I think I would just weep if I saw the glaciers.... I would put on my old boots with their nails, take my crampons and walk around for the sheer joy of it."[10] She got her chance: a reader of the article made it possible for her to revisit her beloved mountain by helicopter when she was eighty-eight years old. She descended from the chopper, leaned on her ice axe, and took some photographs with the camera that had been with her on many of her climbs.

Phyllis Munday died in 1990, almost forty years after her husband. It would be nice to think that what she foresaw in her diary then came true. "When my old body is finished, and dies, my soul will come to a place like this—a mountain meadow, a lake, a lovely woodsy trail, a ridge, a peak, for all this is heaven to me…. It will travel all over the glaciers, which I love so dearly, and the sparkling snow fields, the deep blue crevasses and shining seracs…and sit exalted on my summit, just to look, and look, and love it, deep, deep down in my soul."[11]

<hr/>

In the year of 1927 that saw Phyllis Munday persevere on Mystery Mountain, Geoffrey Blanchet started up the engine on the twenty-five-foot (7.5-metre) gas boat *Caprice* and headed away from his home on Haro Strait for a day's fishing. He was never seen again. His boat was found, but his body never surfaced. The death of this emotional, nervous, intelligent and talented man still in his forties left Muriel Wylie Blanchet a widow with five children, the oldest in her teens, the youngest not yet five. It also changed the course of Muriel Blanchet's life and marked the beginning of adventure. "Destiny rarely follows the pattern we would choose for it and the legacy of death often shapes our lives in ways we could not imagine,"[12] she wrote years later. None of the Blanchets could have imagined the life they would encounter in the next fifteen years, always led onwards by their mother.

Capi—Muriel's nickname, and the designation she preferred—Blanchet was born in 1891, into a well-off Anglo-Quebec family, the middle of three sisters and the tomboy of the family. Her father, a customs broker, was a traveller, disappearing at will to far-off and exotic locales. The girls went to private school, where Muriel soon excelled, setting herself to win the book prizes given for top standing. She seemed set for university, but instead, at eighteen she married bank manager Geoffrey Blanchet. Geoffrey Blanchet became ill when he was in his forties and retired. When he recovered, parents and four children went west in a touring car, arriving eventually on Vancouver Island. Not far from Victoria, they came upon a deserted and marvellous cottage behind a locked gate. They bought it and the land that went with it. A year later, the Blanchets bought the *Caprice* so they could explore the waters near their new home. A fifth child was born. Then Geoffrey Blanchet died, and the saga began.

Every summer for fifteen years, Capi Blanchet rented out her house to a family from Washington and used the money and her own small earnings from freelance writing to underwrite an exploration of the coast. As the children grew older and went off to school, not everyone went north every year. But some always did, and always in the *Caprice*. Years later, Blanchet turned the summers into *The Curve of Time*, probably the best-selling and most-read book ever written about the British Columbia coast. To date, it has gone through two Canadian editions and thirteen printings.

The coast from the southern to the northern tip of Vancouver Island and the opposing mainland is a maze of

Capi Blanchet looks up from her boat at the dock at Shoal Cove in the maze of islands and channels along the mainland coast across from northern Vancouver Island. Thrust into a new way of life by the early death of her husband, Blanchet parlayed an adventuresome spirit and a love for the coast into a series of summer journeys with her family. (PHOTO COURTESY OF JANET BLANCHET)

islands, channels and imposing fjords that angle narrow and northwards through the mountains that rise almost perpendicular to the water. The mainland is a challenge that has never been solved: even now, no roads but logging roads attempt the jagged terrain north of Powell River. The waters are almost as difficult to conquer. Tides, rapids, winds and deep-plunging inlets that admit of no anchorages present constant tests to boaters.

They also bring rewards: unexpected sandy beaches, small lakes just inland, coves and bays where a small boat can lie safe at anchor, the green of the rain forest, the tangled skeins of waterfalls that plunge hundreds of feet down rocky mountainsides and the distant shining glaciers. Now, this coast attracts thousands of boaters, and if you nose into one of the anchorages where Capi Blanchet and her family found solitude, you are likely to find a dozen other boats there before you. Yet there are fewer people living on the coast today than there were when Blanchet did her exploring. The canneries, floating logging camps and marine stores that she visited are almost all gone, and the hardy settlers she met on the narrow margin of soil between the sea and the mountains—planting and harvesting apple orchards, guarding strawberry patches from the deer, growing vegetables to feed themselves and any far-flung neighbours—have long since left, their hard-won gardens returning to the undergrowth. Even the native villages, often temporarily empty when Blanchet saw them as their residents sought out summer fishing or berry-picking grounds, are now permanently deserted, the descendants of the people who once lived there moved to central serviced towns. What Blanchet saw and what fascinated her summer after summer was the living coast, not the tourist coast.

Writing in *Raincoast Chronicles*, Edith Iglauer described Capi Blanchet. "[She] was of medium height, with very fine blonde hair brushed upwards so that it formed a kind of haze around her head. She had a strong rather than a pretty face, round and pleasant. Her normal attire was a pair of khaki shorts, an Indian sweater and sneakers that sometimes had holes in the toes."[13] Iglauer noted that Blanchet had begun wearing shorts long before they were fashionable and some time before they were really acceptable. But fashion and convention were foreign words for Blanchet. She was known as fair-minded but domineering. Her eldest daughter was quoted as saying that "She was a challenge for any child, but slightly dampening. She could do anything that men did, and still be feminine."[14]

Her coastal adventures were particularly suited to her temperament and her abilities. Many a person who knew her spoke of her mechanical skills, good to have when you are nautical miles from anywhere and anyone and your engine seizes up. "Engines were invented and reared by men," wrote Blanchet. "They are used to being sworn at, and just take advantage of you; if you are polite to them — you get absolutely nowhere."[15] On one occasion, the engine stopped just as dark fell, and Blanchet had to row five miles (eight kilometres) in the dinghy at night, towing the boat with its cargo of sleeping children behind. Her description of trying to repair the engine the next day, while the children played on the beach where she had sent them to keep them out of her way, will be familiar to anyone who has ever worked on a boat engine:

"I sat on my heels, cursing softly when the wrench slipped and took a chunk off my knuckle. Finally the spark plug co-operated and came out with the porcelain still intact. Then I stuck the screwdriver through the hole and felt around for No. 1 piston. That piston seemed quite inert…but after some turns of the flywheel it came up on top. No. 1 valve should be either opening or closing, I wasn't sure which. The only valve I could see through the small hole was doing either one or the other" and Blanchet continued her engine exploration. "The magneto must be the key to the whole thing. The engine was an old four-cylinder Kermath with a low-tension magneto. The distributor was on the face of the magneto, and the wires from the sparkplugs led down to the distributor….(Dots for a very long time.)"[16] Blanchet diagnosed the fault—too easily, she thought, until she realized that her subconscious had probably been at work all night. She put a nail in the place of the errant pin in the coupling, securing it with electrical tape. She pulled the crank—and the engine backfired so violently it had the children shouting on shore. She worked out what went wrong, the engine purred and she shook hands with her subconscious.

The Capi Blanchet who is revealed through her book was adept, calm, in command, ever able to conquer her fear when her children's safety was at stake. On one visit to Princess Louisa Inlet, the family climbed up beside Chatterbox Falls, the 122-foot (thirty-seven-metre) cascade that has now made the inlet famous. On hands and knees, they edged towards the log that crossed the stream above the falls. They began to romp across a sheet of green moss that covered the steep rock. Blanchet suddenly felt the moss begin to slip. "I shouted to the children not to move, and worked my way up a crack of bare granite, pushing John ahead of me—then anchored myself to a bush. I made the children crawl up, one by one, to where there were some bushes to hang onto. From there, they worked up to a tree."[17] One of the older girls held onto a bush, then lowered herself so the young boy could catch her feet and pull himself up. Blanchet then held onto her daughter's feet, and sprang upwards to where she too could clutch a bush. Below them all, the sheet of moss lost its grip on the rock, then slowly slid over the edge. Though Blanchet must have been frightened, she admitted only to being shaken and immediately began to devise a way to get herself and her children back home to the boat. That way involved using a bear trail: the sixsome strode along, singing loudly, and returned safely to the beach.

The Blanchet who emerged from her own words was also sensitive to the many-layered past of the coast, and the way the past slid into present and future. She visited many of the old coastal native villages and heard the ancient Kwakwaka'wakw singing to her from the longhouses and grave boxes that were disintegrating in the trees. She also learned the tides and currents of the coast. Now, many coastal cruising guides point out difficulties, anchorages and routes. Then, there was only the coastal pilot, the charts and the diaries of the explorers who had come this way a century and a half before. Blanchet kept a copy of Captain George Vancouver's diary aboard the *Caprice* and Vancouver's comments and explorations formed a backdrop for her own.

The children grew up—the youngest three schooled at home in the winters—and went away for further schooling, for jobs, for their own lives. The last of the cruising summers was in the early 1940s. World War II interrupted their idylls, and Blanchet's youngest child joined the army. The touring summers over, Blanchet continued to live at the cottage on southern Vancouver Island. After the war, she sold the *Caprice*. The boat was hauled up on the ways for repairs when the boat works burned down, taking the *Caprice* with them.

In these years ashore, daughters- and sons-in-law who married into the family came to know and respect Capi Blanchet's strength and independence—and sometimes be amused by her eccentricities. "She was a serious-minded person, very determined, never particularly light-hearted," recalled Janet Blanchet, who married Blanchet's youngest son, David. "She didn't worry about anyone else's opinion of her."[18]

Living alone at Curteis Point, Capi Blanchet developed her own routine. "She felt she didn't really need heat in the morning in summer," said Janet, "so she didn't want to turn on the oil stove till after lunch. She usually had a poached egg on toast for breakfast. So she took her electric iron and balanced it upside down on two good-sized rocks, put the pan on top and poached her eggs that way.

"She liked fish but couldn't stand the smell of it cooking. One day when we were there, she didn't want to wash the plates that smelled of fish, so she walked down to the point with them, to put them in the ocean at low tide, so the tide would come and the crabs would clean them."[19] But the tide wasn't right, so she left the plates there for later and forgot about them; when she returned, plates and cutlery had disappeared. She immediately posted an ad in the local paper, saying that she had seen the people who had taken them and demanding their return. She got back her plates.

She was a practical woman. Finding a valuable samurai sword in the attic, she took it out to cut back the broom and brush along her path. She put it down there when she went in for tea; it too disappeared, but this time, her property did not come back.

A doctor advised her to find a drier climate, for the wet and chill of the island were not doing her emphysema any good. Blanchet had no intention of moving. Instead, she sat with her head as far as she could get it into her oil stove for twenty minutes every day and declared that to be her dry climate.

"She was a sterling character," Janet Blanchet summed up. "I don't think she ever let anyone down knowingly. She was a rock. She had integrity."[20]

By the late 1950s, Blanchet had completed her classic book, and sent it off to Blackwoods in London, a company that had bought some of her freelance writing for their magazine. Blackwoods agreed to publish it, but the publishing was something of an anti-climax: few copies of the book ever made their way to Vancouver Island. Undeterred, she started work on another book. In September of 1961 she was found at her typewriter, dead of a heart attack. She was seventy years old.

Those who had known her would not let her memory and her writing die. In 1968, the first Canadian edition of *The Curve of Time* was published. That edition went through seven printings, as Capi Blanchet's beautifully crafted stories of the coast found thousands of fans. A second edition was published in 1990; six printings later, it still regularly finds it way onto coastal best-seller lists, testimony to the remarkable life and talent of this determined adventurer.

Notes:

1 "Phyllis Munday—Expeditions to Mystery Mountain, 1926-1933," *In the Western Mountains: Early Mountaineering in British Columbia*, Sound Heritage, VIII/4 (Victoria: Provincial Archives of British Columbia, 1980), p. 60.

2 Munday, Don. *The Unknown Mountain* (Lake Louise: Coyote Books, 1993), p. 105.

3 *Canadian Alpine Journal*, 1909.

4 *In the Western Mountains*, p. 24.

5 as quoted in Smith, Cyndi. *Off the Beaten Track: Women Adventurers and Mountaineers in Western Canada* (Jasper: Coyote Books, 1989), p. 165.

6 "The First Ascent of Mount Robson by Lady Members," *Canadian Alpine Journal*, 1924.

7 *In the Western Mountains*, p. 61.

8 *The Unknown Mountain*, foreword by Angus M. Gunn, *Behind the Unknown Mountain*, p. xxv.

9 Ibid.

10 *Beautiful British Columbia Magazine*, Summer 1982.

11 as quoted in Gunn, *Behind the Unknown Mountain*, p. xxx.

12 Blanchet, M. Wylie. *The Curve of Time* (Vancouver: Whitecap Books, 1990), p. 161.

13 Iglauer, Edith. *Raincoast Chronicles #8*, pp. 40-44.

14 Ibid.

15 Blanchet. *The Curve of Time*, p. 106.

16 Ibid., pp. 106-7.

17 Ibid., pp. 16-17.

18 Interview with Janet Blanchet, May 24, 2000.

19 Ibid.

20 Ibid.

THERE IS
ETERNAL NATURE

A Love of Place

At first glance, they seem to have little in common. Gilean Douglas was a writer, a traveller, a charming woman who had no children but many friends. Annie Rae Arthur ran a nursery business from an isolated homestead, was known more for her determination than her charm, and gave birth to eleven children. Yet their lives have surprising similarities. Each was an only child, doted on or dominated by a father who was the central figure in her young life. Each married four times—though for very different reasons. Each was a dedicated gardener. Most important, the key element in each life was a fierce and fundamental connection to the places where they lived.[1]

Ada Annie Rae Arthur was born in California in June of 1888. Her father was ever a traveller. Before she was twenty, she had lived in England, South Africa, Alberta and Manitoba, fetching up in Vancouver after her father trained as a veterinarian and set up a clinic on Canada's Pacific coast.

Her father taught her to shoot and trap, raising her almost as a boy until she was seven or eight years old. The family's frequent travels made her something of a loner, learning early how to live independently of others. In her teens, she worked as a stenographer and an office manager in Winnipeg. In Vancouver, she continued her office work, and also helped in her father's clinic. Into that clinic one day with his terrier came Willie Rae Arthur, a Scot fifteen years older than Annie, a slight and attractive man of great verve. Annie was enchanted; the family was impressed by Willie's background, for he came from an upper-middle-class family that included people of influence in Vancouver and Scotland. The two were married in 1909. A few months later, Annie's mother died.

The photographs of the young Annie show her, girl and woman, as handsome, with a direct, challenging stare from wide eyes. It's a strong, almost masculine face, not cute or pretty, but captivating. Everything about Annie's later life was to prove her strength. Willie was her weakness. A fondness for drink, a liking for smoking opium in Chinatown, a preference for play over work, all led Willie into trouble. When the drink and drugs began to endanger Willie's life, his family decided he must be removed from temptation. A friend of Annie's father told them of a place on the west coast of Vancouver Island where the family could live far from Vancouver's temptations. In 1915, Willie and Annie, four months pregnant, with their five- and three-year-old sons and an infant daughter, went by schooner to Boat Basin in Hesquiat Harbour, an isolated spot north of Tofino.

There, they pre-empted 160 acres (sixty-five hectares) of not very promising land, heavily treed and much of it boggy. A Hesquiat Indian village was at the head of the harbour; a few non-natives lived at the harbour mouth. They had only one set of close neighbours. When the woman died the following year, her husband left and they had none.

The work of homesteading began: cutting down trees, blasting or burning stumps. Much of the work fell to Annie; Willie was better at sketching, singing, rolling cigarettes from the pages of the family Bible and rowing off to Tofino to swap yarns with other expatriate Brits who had fetched up as far west as they could go in Canada. Between them, they cleared some seven acres (three hectares) of good soil and built paths and drainage ditches. Rae Arthur then set to work on her dream, a garden of vegetables to feed the family, and flowers, bulbs, tubers and ornamental trees to feed her heart and her imagination and to allow her to establish a mail-order nursery business.

Ada Annie and Willie lived together at Boat Basin for twenty-one years, with an ever-increasing family. Children were born in 1915, 1917, 1920, 1923 and 1927. Three other children died shortly after birth, in 1926, 1930 and 1931. Sometimes a doctor or Indian midwife came to help Rae Arthur give birth. Often she was alone.

There was a sense after World War I that the whole west coast of the island would attract more settlers, that prosperity was not far off and that isolation would diminish as transportation inevitably improved. That did not happen. Instead, the Rae Arthurs adapted to the isolation. In 1923, they began building a new house to replace the old shack that had housed their growing family. Soon, one of its four rooms was filled with Rae Arthur's stock for a small store and the post office that she had wangled from the government when the former post office at Hesquiat Village closed. A monthly stipend from the post office and remittance payments from Willie's well-off sister in Scotland helped to supply what Annie couldn't grow, raise or shoot: hay and oats for the livestock, flour, sugar, building supplies and fencing.

There were chickens aplenty, for eggs and meat; goats supplied meat and milk. Rabbits, ducks and geese filled out the menagerie. The skills of hunting and trapping that Rae Arthur had learned early from her father were put to good use at Boat Basin. She became known as "Cougar Annie," for the thirty, fifty or seventy—reports varied—cougars she had killed for the bounty paid on these west-coast wild cats. She also sold their pelts and bottled the meat. She trapped mink and marten, and shot bear and wolves. Always close with her money, she bartered and delayed whenever payment was required.

Her most important work was her nursery. In her ragged but well-organized garden, she grew tubers, perennials, bulbs and ornamental and fruit trees, becoming best known for her dahlias. Her plants went out across Canada, and she had a continuing correspondence with many of those who ordered from her. In later years, her children recalled her as the stern parent, their father as the one who was always ready with a joke or a song. In 1923, authorities, alerted to this family living almost wild and without schooling, came to take her three oldest children to school in Vancouver. The three did not see their parents again for several years. The younger five children were educated by correspondence lessons.

In 1936, Willie rowed out into the harbour to go fishing. Somehow, he fell overboard and drowned. Now the work at Boat Basin fell completely on Annie and the three children who still lived at Boat Basin. Looking at the work required by her business, and by the fact of living in isolation, she decided she needed a new man about the place. Straightforward as ever, she advertised for one, in the *Western Producer* and in the *Winnipeg Free Press*.

Several men replied. She invited one or two to come and visit, but none took the proffered bait. Then in 1940, Scot George Campbell arrived. The couple was married shortly thereafter. But four years later she was a widow again. Campbell died when he was hit in the thigh by a bullet and bled to death. The official report classified the shot as an accident, but rumour surrounded the event. Did Campbell beat and threaten Rae Arthur? Was he cleaning the gun when it went off or did she kill him? No one knew but Annie Rae Arthur—though one could conjecture that Rae Arthur, a superb shot, might have made a cleaner job of any intentional shooting.

By now, only one son still lived at Boat Basin, though three others continued to visit; the girls had all moved away from the isolation and constant work. In 1945, Ada Annie Rae Arthur was fifty-seven and faced with the labour of both nursery and general upkeep. She wrote to Esau Arnold, who had replied to the original husband-hunting advertisement but had then become ill. Arnold, a Saskatchewan farmer in his sixties, arrived in Boat Basin and married Rae Arthur in 1947. That same year, son Laurie drowned in Hesquiat Harbour.

Seven years later, the accident jinx struck again. Arnold cut his leg badly, gangrene set in, and he died early in 1955, perhaps from a subsequent heart attack. Rae Arthur advertised once more, this time attracting Robert Culver and his three children. This relationship looked promising: Culver quickly became fond of Rae Arthur. But he feared that isolation and distance from medical care could badly affect his children and moved on. In 1956, Rae Arthur's son Tommy moved back to Boat Basin.

Rae Arthur's fame as a cougar hunter attracted attention up and down the coast. In 1957, *Vancouver Sun* writer Alex McGillivray dropped by to interview her. In an article headlined, "Death for 62 cougars—Woman Sniper Kills 'Cats,'" he reported asking her if she were not afraid, living virtually alone in a wilderness where cougar and bear abounded. "The clear blue eyes of this remarkable woman reflected surprise at the question," he wrote. "'I love to meet a cougar if I've got a gun,' she said. 'If they'd leave my goats alone, I'd leave them alone.' The last cougar that raided Mrs. Arnold's goat barn killed nine goats. Now he is dead. It took her three days to get the big orange-coloured beast into a trap."

McGillivray noted that Rae Arthur was reputed to have killed sixty-two cougars and eighty bears with her 30-30 Winchester rifle. Sight fast and aim for the chest was her recipe for downing a cougar. "The woman who gave me this advice Friday offered it as she would a cookie recipe. Fortunately, it is a recipe of sudden death she has used with fantastic success since the 1920s."[2]

In about 1960, now seventy-two, Rae Arthur married for a fourth time, to sixty-year-old George Lawson. This was no better a choice than her previous husbands had been. Lawson reportedly stole from her and beat her. He left in about 1967, probably driven off by Rae Arthur. Robert Culver's children were by now grown and he had never forgotten Rae Arthur. He returned and became a constant in her life. Though they never married, they were good and close friends. By 1971, the cold and damp at Boat Basin was more than Culver could stand, and he moved away, returning every summer as long as he could. He died in 1983.

By 1980, Ada Annie Rae Arthur had lived at Boat Basin for more than sixty years. She still ran her nursery business, specializing in dahlias because the tubers were simpler to grow and easier to ship than other plant material. She had outlived two more of her sons: George, a linesman in Tofino, died of a heart attack in 1973; Frank drowned in 1979. Tommy stayed on in his own cabin. A logging road was built past the place to a nearby logging camp, and the loggers adopted Rae Arthur, calling in to check on her and bringing her supplies.

Rae Arthur's blazing blue eyes were now almost blind and the property had become too much for her. The garden began to fall into disrepair; the beds, always untidy, were invaded by native plants. Though the family tried to convince her to leave Boat Basin, she would not be swayed: this was the one place in the world where she belonged. In 1981 she sold her property on the condition she could live there until she died and a couple was hired to help her. Almost housebound, her garden overgrown, she was finally persuaded to leave in 1983. Taken by logging truck and float plane to Port Alberni, she died there in 1985. Her ashes were brought back to Boat Basin and scattered over her garden.

Gilean Douglas married four times, once an unintentional —though arguably careless—bigamy. She struggled with her health for all of her life and her involvements with men for half of it and was rarely sure how she would make enough to live on. A writer from age seven, she rebelled against what she thought society expected from women and found her salvation in her writing and in her strong attachment to nature. Three things and three things only were steadfast in her life, she wrote: "nature, my writing, and somewhere, somehow, a steady belief that in spite of all our many backslidings, we do go on and up.... Friendship and love can only go so far; in the end there is only ourselves. For me there is also eternal nature."[3]

Gilean Douglas was born in 1900 in Toronto. Like Rae Arthur, she was an only child. Her parents were well-off and very much part of Toronto society. Her mother died when she was six; from that point on, life in the big Toronto house revolved around the young girl, who later described herself as a princess in a castle. Her father doted on her, the housekeeper cared for her and the other servants did her bidding. Her later memories included sitting with her father in the library while he read from the well-stocked shelves and she

Gilean Douglas found a long-sought home when she claimed a retreat in the Cascade Mountains northeast of Hope. (PHOTO COURTESY OF GILLIAN MILTON)

did her homework. When he travelled, he wrote to her every day. But William Douglas was an alcoholic with heart problems. He died just before Douglas's sixteenth birthday.

The princess did not become the pauper overnight, but her privileged life was at an end. She hated the boarding school she was sent to. The relatives she stayed with in school holidays were, to her mind, unsympathetic. They were certainly poorer than her parents had been, and though her father had left Douglas his entire estate, it would take five years for that estate to be settled. Eventually that inheritance provided enough money to underwrite the freedom that she craved. Always determined to be a writer, Douglas got a job as a reporter with the *Toronto News* at the age of nineteen. The next few years brought job changes, flirtations, boyfriends. Describing herself as a little pretty, with straight brown hair, a high forehead, good eyes and mouth and complexion, a passionate female with a New England conscience, she possessed an encompassing smile and considerable charm. She couldn't resist involvements with several men at the same time: "I hauled myself dripping out of one mud puddle only to fall backwards into another."[4]

Then in 1921, she met Cecil Rhodes, a craggy-faced, strong-jawed charming man known as Slim, who seemed to be her dream man. The two were soon married, with Rhodes taking Douglas's last name at her insistence. The newlyweds embarked on an adventuresome cross-America jaunt in a Model T Ford. Two years of carefree travelling and writing followed. When a chronic thyroid condition flared up, complicated by heart problems, Gilean Douglas was forced to spend seven months in a Florida hospital. Released, she returned home to Toronto alone. The marriage to Slim was over. Later in life, Douglas decided he had married her for her money. "It would have been the best thing for both of us," she wrote, "if we had never met."[5]

Through the rest of the decade, Douglas continued free-lancing, flirting and travelling. In 1929, assuming her first husband was dead, she married again—only to have Slim reappear. When he walked in, her second husband walked out—and Slim disappeared once more. In 1933, she divorced Slim in Reno so she could marry her new beau, mining engineer Eric Altherr. They were soon unhappy and separated in 1937. Douglas's biographers Andrea Lebowitz and Gillian Milton sum up Douglas's difficulties with marriage: "She fiercely desired someone for whom she would be the absolute centre of existence. Since the death of her father, she had sought a worthy object of love—but not at the price of independence. Therein lay the rub. To find a mate who would respect her ambitions and needs yet provide a strong and unquestioning love was a tall order. She was willing to trade quite a bit of autonomy for a partner, but having made the trade, she began to chafe under the terms, and hers were never happy or long relationships. She later opined that had she been a man, the conflicts in her personality would have been tolerated and she would have been able to pursue her public career without sacrificing her personal desires."[6]

Learning little from experience, she got involved with yet another lover, Ted Geppert, a married man who worked at the same mine as Altherr. Geppert and Douglas moved to Vancouver, and Geppert went placer mining in the Cascade Mountains east of Vancouver. In 1939, Douglas went to visit him at his cabin. It was a fateful moment: Douglas had found a place that she could call home:

For more than twenty years I had been homeless. It was not that I had no roof over my head during that time, but that I had too many. Roofs of relatives' houses, schools, boardinghouses, apartments, duplexes, tents, automobiles, trains, shops, summer cottages. But there had never been a home.... there had never been a garden. Not a real garden.

Then one day as I was fishing a strange western river, I came to a deep pool where the trout and the steelhead were both wise and wary. I flicked a red admiral across the dark green water, hoping for a Dolly Varden, and then I looked up at my surroundings. My right arm dropped slowly to my side, and the top of my rod broke the surface of the pool. I stood perfectly still and was not conscious that I breathed, for there, right across from me, gazing into my face with its deep-set windows, was—my home.[7]

She moved into this cabin in the Coquihalla, east of Hope and the Fraser Valley, where the huge cedars and firs and the rain of the coastal forest ease into the beginnings of British Columbia's dry country. She worked steadily to fashion a bright, homey wilderness retreat. Outside, she dug and planted and weeded, to create a garden both practical—for the vegetables that helped sustain her—and beautiful, with drifts of flowers across the rocks and below the trees. The cabin and its surroundings became her haven. "It was the great moment in my life when I waded the Teal River with my packboard on my back and stood at last on my own ground. I can never describe the feeling that surged up inside me then. I stood now where I should have been always. I felt kinship in everything around me, and the long city years of noises and faces were just fading photographs."[8]

She delighted in the cabin's isolation, reachable by a spur line from the railway, then by a platform that ran across the river on a cable. "All that I do here is not work but delight," she wrote. Snapshots of her life might have shown her sitting on green moss, leaning on a log, eating peanut butter sandwiches and typing away on her latest work; or just before dark, going up to a knoll, sitting with her back to an old cedar, and looking down on her river; or, on a hot day, paddling around in "big rubber boots and nothing else."[9]

From this sojourn came two books. *River for My Sidewalk* was published in 1953 under the pseudonym of Grant Madison, for her publisher was convinced that no such epic of wilderness living would be believed if written in a woman's name. It was reissued in 1984, finally under her own name. *Silence Is My Homeland* was not published until 1978; it was awarded the National Writers' Club prize for best unpublished manuscript submitted in that year. Both books resonate with her love for this wild region and with the knowledge garnered in decades of broad-based reading. She looked with great fondness on a life regulated by the sun and the weather, without electricity or the comforts she had come to think were necessary. The coyotes, mule deer, black bear and cougars delighted her, though she grieved for the huge trees and beaver that no longer were part of her wilderness.

She lived on fish, a little wild meat, wild berries, forest and clearing plants, vegetables from her own garden, and whatever staples she chose to pack in from the railway spur that ran a day's hike from her cabin. "Working out my garden-to-be on paper," she wrote, "I have that splendid feeling of material self-sufficiency which is such a vital part of wilderness life. If all the stores closed and all the railroads stopped running I could still manage."[10]

Visitors came to see her, and for the first few years, Geppert spent some time each year at the cabin. But this relationship, too, was falling apart. Though she wrote him long loving letters, saying how much she missed him, he somehow annoyed her when he was there. In 1941, she bought the property from him and their relationship later ended.

She wrote volumes at the cabin, books, articles, poems and essays. Happier than she had ever been, she explained what it was like to live here, so close to the earth. "It is the most wonderful thing that could happen to anyone. The hours in my Cascade mountain valley don't run by clock or whistle; they are regulated much more grandly by the sun and moon.... The boss of my work is the weather...All weather is good because there is always something good to be done. All time is good—but there is never enough of it for all the things I want to do. Yes, that I *want* to do. I cannot remember performing one task here that I did not thoroughly enjoy."[11]

It was her paradise. And then it was her paradise lost. Early in May of 1947, her cabin caught fire and was destroyed. She had scant minutes to rescue what was most important to her: her manuscripts, her typewriter, anything that had to do with her work as a writer. She saved a few of her books and a few armloads of clothes. Everything else, including several manuscripts in preparation and the research for them, was devoured by the flames.

Her idyll was over. Now forty-seven, she knew she was not healthy and strong enough to rebuild, carrying in on her back every board and window and book—if indeed she could afford it. She moved in with friends on the coast, and, bereft, considered what to do next. She had an ongoing relationship with Philip Major, who wanted to divorce his wife and marry Douglas. Douglas was more hesitant. In the end, she bought a place on Cortes Island with the last of her dwindling inheritance, planning that Major would renovate the house and cottage there and that she would support him from her writing. Like many another plan of Douglas's that involved a man, it didn't work. The two married in 1949, with Major taking Douglas's name, but the marriage was again a failure. They separated in 1953 and divorced in 1955. That marriage was her last serious love relationship.

Although she began by missing her Cascade mountains and rivers dreadfully, within a year or two she fell in love with her new retreat. Cortes was not as isolated as the mountain cabin, nor was the surrounding terrain as majestic, but it had its allure. The island was reachable only by steamship—no ferry existed at that time—and Douglas's property was far from the boat dock. Now began more than forty years of living happily on her own, except for her beloved cats and the birds and creatures of the surrounding woodland. Douglas continued to write. She became widely known on Vancouver Island for her weekly nature rambles column in the *Victoria Times Colonist*. She involved herself in the politics of Cortes Island, often acting as island residents' spokesperson, working to protect its natural environment, and with local and provincial women's groups.

Between 1955 and 1993, ten of her books of poetry and nature writing were published. As she grew older, photographs of her still showed that wide smile, that zest for life. In her later years, she was helped by a young man who lived on her property and she made friends with many others on the island. Her health declined and she had increasing money problems: her freelancing brought in barely enough to survive. Finally, she was able to sell the property, with a covenant protecting it against despoliation, thus gaining enough money to live on and make her last years easier.

Gilean Douglas died at home on October 31, 1993, two days after she announced that she had completed the book she was working on. Her ashes were interred on the property she had grown to love.

Notes:

[1] Interestingly, as this chapter was being written in the fall of 1999, full and excellent biographies of each of these women were published: *Cougar Annie's Garden*, by Margaret Horsfield (Nanaimo: Salal Books, 1999), weaves the story of Rae Arthur's life through the story of the place where she lived and the garden she created. *Gilean Douglas: Writing Nature, Finding Home*, by Andrea Lebowitz and Gillian Milton (Victoria: Sono Nis, 1999), is both a biography and a collection of some of Douglas's best work.

[2] *Vancouver Sun*, October 19, 1957.

[3] Gilean Douglas collection, University of British Columbia Special Collections, File 30-17.

[4] Ibid., File 6-12.

[5] Ibid., *A February Face*, unfinished autobiography.

[6] Lebowitz, Andrea, and Milton, Gillian. *Gilean Douglas: Writing Nature, Finding Home* (Victoria: Sono Nis, 1999), p. 48.

[7] Douglas, Gilean. *Silence Is My Homeland: Life on Teal River* (Harrisburg, Penn.: Stackpole Books, 1978), p. 9.

[8] Ibid., p. 14.

[9] Gilean Douglas collection, File 30-17.

[10] Douglas, Gilean. *River for my Sidewalk* (Victoria: Sono Nis, 1984), p. 27.

[11] Ibid., p. 12.

Women Not to Be Deterred

New York City in the 1920s hummed with the comings and goings of four million residents, three-quarters of them immigrants or the children of immigrants. Men, women and children crowded the streets of the east side, rode the newly built subways, lived in the tenements and worked in rapidly growing industries, many slaving in sweatshops.

More than a third of the 17 million people who arrived at the American immigration centre on Ellis Island between 1890 and 1930 came from central and eastern Europe to swell rapidly growing Russian, Polish and other immigrant communities. The Russian Revolution of 1917 and the subsequent civil war chased many Russians from their homes and native land; New York was the destination for a large number of these émigrés. Though they had little to do with the roar of the twenties — the speakeasies and jazz clubs that were part of the fast life of the cities — most were reasonably content with their new country.

Lillian Alling was not. Like much about Alling's life, the facts of her birth and childhood are unconfirmed. She was probably born shortly after 1900 in Russia, or possibly Poland. She came to the United States after the revolution, probably entering with thousands of her fellow Russians at Ellis Island. Some say she was one of the many upper-class and aristocratic Russians who fled Russia at that time; descriptions of her suggest she was well educated and well spoken. One report suggested that she had been sent by her family to find them all a new home, and that, while she was travelling, her family was thrown into exile in Siberia—but this report may have been romantic invention.

Whoever she was, however she arrived in America, she was soon convinced that she did not want to stay. Somehow, she would return to Russia. She never told anyone who recorded her response why she wanted to return, other than

Linesman Charlie Janze and his fellow telegraph workers knew what they were talking about when they warned Lillian Alling of the dangers that could be expected by anyone walking the Telegraph Trail. Here, Janze is shown near the Nass-Skeena divide, on the trail in winter. (LANCE BURDON, PHOTOGRAPHER; BCA D-07630)

to say that she felt alone and unwelcome, despite the large numbers of people in her same circumstances. Perhaps it was the bustle and strangeness of the city. Perhaps it was some more compelling or frightening incident. Perhaps she yearned to rejoin a sweetheart or her family. Whatever impelled her, though, must have been strong motivation indeed, for it drove her to undertake an almost impossible trek, to brave hardship and jail and to continue on when saner heads urged caution.

Alling is one of a handful of western women whose legends grow with time, and whose stories are still told around the coffee cups and beer glasses of the regions where they lived or travelled. These women lived lives of pure determination, often in almost total isolation from other people. Some called them eccentric; some called them crazy. They were as little interested in such judgements as they were in other people's advice on what they should do or how they should live. Regardless of the cost, they lived as they wished.

Lillian Alling worked as a maid in New York, a job that did not allow her to save enough money to buy a ticket aboard a ship returning to Europe. Blocked from the simplest way home, she began to develop another plan. In the New York Public Library, she spread out on the table in front of her maps of the United States, Canada and Siberia. She decided she would walk home, north through British Columbia, the Yukon and Alaska, somehow across the Bering Strait, then through Siberia, the Ural Mountains and home.

The small hill of information available about Lillian Alling's odyssey is dwarfed by the mountain that is unknown. Probably in the spring of 1927, she set out on foot from New York, dressed in a stout skirt and shod in sturdy shoes. She seems to have aroused no particular comment among the many who travelled the highways newly built for the ever more popular automobile, or on the old wagon roads or railway tracks, though many must have wondered about this woman who walked alone and steadily west. Later, she said that she had been through Winnipeg, which suggests that she followed a Canadian route along the transcontinental train tracks across the prairies and perhaps through Jasper to Prince George and Smithers, in British Columbia's northwest.

The first absolute fact in the trek of Lillian Alling is that on September 10, 1927, she walked up to a lonely cabin north of Hazelton, the home of Yukon telegraph lineman Bill Blackstock. Amazed at the story he heard, in awe of her tenacity in reaching this far, he was nonetheless quickly

This photo shows the Telegraph Trail snaking up the hill from the Sheep Creek Cabin, on Lillian Alling's route north. Alling refused to let the rough trail, the weather or the possibility of starvation deter her from her trek. (BCA A-04962)

convinced that she would die if she continued her journey north into the rapidly approaching winter weather. He telegraphed the provincial police officer in Hazelton, some sixty miles (ninety-five kilometres) south, and asked for advice. George Wyman, a young police constable, set out immediately for Blackstock's Cabin 2. There, he found a woman about five foot five (165 centimetres) and "thin as a wisp," wearing running shoes and carrying a knapsack that contained sandwiches, tea, a comb, and a few other personal effects.

Guy Lawrence, a forty-year veteran of life on the Telegraph Trail, later described this section of the trail in winter: "Sudden heavy falls of snow would bring the line down in several places, over perhaps a seventy-mile stretch. Between Hazelton and Telegraph Creek, some sections were subjected to phenomenal precipitation during the long winter months. Crews at stations at fairly high altitudes made a habit of erecting long poles beside their small refuge cabins to help find them. Many of the mountain passes were subject to snowslides, which snapped poles and buried the wire under sixty feet of snow for the remainder of the winter."[1] Yet, underequipped as she was, as ignorant as she could be of the hazards that faced her, Alling told Wyman she was absolutely determined to continue north.

Wyman would not let her go to what he thought was certain death. He decided to take her with him to Hazelton. Surprisingly, she put up no fight, turning back dumbly to accompany him. Once back in Hazelton, she told Wyman the bare bones of her story, and declared that she would, somehow, continue. Said Wyman many years later, "She was the most determined person I'd ever met."[2] He conferred with his superior officer, Sgt. W.J. Service, who also warned Alling of the severe winter conditions ahead and told her she would in all probability freeze to death. She was not dissuaded. The men knew that the moment that she was released, she would be back on the Telegraph Trail.

Service decided that he would arrest Alling for her own protection. She was searched; she carried two ten-dollar bills, a reasonably sure defence against any charge of vagrancy. Arraigned before a justice of the peace on September 21, she was convicted instead of carrying an offensive weapon, the eighteen-inch (half-metre) metal bar she had with her to protect herself, not against wild animals, but against men. One account suggests that she was asked four times if she had anything to say. At the fourth, she let fly four obscene expletives. The justice of the peace fined her twenty-five dollars, a sum she did not have. In lieu of payment, she was sentenced to two months in Oakalla Prison, near Vancouver, a ruling that would accomplish the lawmen's objective of keeping her off the trail in winter.

She duly served her time. Once she was released, prison staff found her a job for the rest of the winter at a Vancouver restaurant, where she saved as much money as she could. Come spring, she set out once more. On July 19, she arrived at Smithers, where a policeman again tried to dissuade her from her trek. She declined, but she did promise that she would check in at each of the cabins on the Telegraph Trail. This she did. Several weeks later, linesmen Jim Christie and Charlie Janze watched in amazement as she walked into the clearing where their two small cabins stood, her face badly swollen from insect bites, windburned and sunburned, slumping from exhaustion and lack of food, her clothes almost in tatters. Yet she would not turn back.

Since they knew they could not dissuade her, they tried to help. Christie gave her his cabin. Over the next three days and nights, she ate well, slept indoors and began to recuperate. Janze gave her a pair of breeches and two shirts, a felt hat and a pair of boots that would fit her smaller feet with the aid of two pairs of woollen socks. Then Christie set out with Alling towards the Nass summit and Cabin 9 on the trail. Meanwhile, linesman Scotty Ogilvie left Cabin 9 to come south to meet her. He never arrived. Trying to cross a river in flood, he tumbled in, hit his head on a snag and drowned. His fellow linesman at Cabin 9 found him the next day, his body wedged against a waterlogged cottonwood tree. Ogilvie was buried nearby. When Alling passed this way the next day, it is said that she left behind a small bunch of wildflowers.

The knowledge that death came easily in the north had no more impact on Alling than all the warnings of those who had tried to dissuade her. She was walking to Russia. She would continue unless her own death intervened. Her determination —and her refusal to understand the possible problems—so impressed one of the linesmen that he gave her his black and white husky dog, Bruno, to provide company and to carry her pack. But, insisted the linesman, she must not let Bruno run free near the Iskut River, where poison traps were set for wolverine. It is thought that the dog must have eluded her, for another linesman saw it die near the river.

Alling continued on from Iskut, arriving in Atlin in August, where she bought a pair of shoes so she could walk ever farther northward. At Tagish, in the Yukon, a local resident took her across the river in a boat. At Carcross, she had a meal in a hotel. North of Carcross, a local couple overtook her on the road, and offered her a ride in their car. She rode with them as far as they were going, then resumed her lonely travels. On the last day of August, the *Whitehorse Star* announced that "a woman giving the name of Lillian Alling walked into town Monday evening and registered at the Regina Hotel. Lillian was not given much to speaking but as near as can be gathered from information she gave at different places she had walked from Hazelton to Whitehorse."[3]

The newspaper named her the Mystery Woman, and tracked her further progress. She had, said one of the stories, left Whitehorse carrying a loaf of bread as her only food. As she journeyed on, various locals ferried her across the rivers that barred her way. On one occasion, she stayed through a bad storm with a survey party, then continued on down the Yukon River in a small boat. On October 5, she reached Dawson City, some 5,000 miles (8000 kilometres) from her starting point a year and a half earlier in New York. She stayed there for the winter, working as a waitress and repairing the boat she had bought for her continued journey down the Yukon. When the ice broke up in the spring, she followed the river towards the Bering Sea, steering her small craft through the last remaining floating ice.

What happened to her after that is a matter of conjecture, based on flimsy pieces of conflicting hearsay evidence. Lillian Alling's story quickly became a northern legend, with different versions of the end of her story sworn to by those who said they had met her along the way, or had met someone who had met her, or seen her, or heard of her fate.

One version suggested that she had not gone north at all. A policeman who had met her on her journey said he had received a letter from her, saying she had gone to Telegraph Creek to find her Russian sweetheart. On finding he had departed, she married another man. But there is too much evidence that she did indeed go north; the policeman must have confused her with someone else. Some versions report that she had the stuffed hide of the dog that had been poisoned with her all the way, perhaps at the top of her backpack, perhaps in the cart she was said at one point to have trundled behind her. But her ability to preserve a decaying hide while persisting on her way north must be doubted. Some say that an Inuit man saw her footprints at the edge of a river near the Bering Sea and that she must undoubtedly have drowned there. Others say she found someone to take her across the Bering Sea by boat, then disappeared into Siberia.

We want a happy ending for Lillian Alling. A California man, who visited Siberia in 1965, wrote to a magazine to say he thought he had found one. While in Siberia, he had spoken with a friend there. The friend said that, as a boy of fourteen or fifteen, he lived on the Siberian shore of the Bering Strait. He saw a woman and three Inuit men whom he recognized as being from the Diomede Islands in the strait arrive on the waterfront. The woman said she had come from America, where she had been unable to find friends or make a living. She had decided to walk home to Russia and had done so. On her route, she said, no one had lifted as much as a finger to help her in any way.[4] If this was indeed Lillian Alling, her comments would surely have come as a great disappointment to the many people who had helped her on her journey.

The letter writer said his friend told him all this had happened in the fall of 1930. But neither he nor anyone else living knows for certain how Lillian Alling's odyssey ended.

⁜

Alling's brief time in the west created a legend larger than her life. The legend of Chiwid rests on a much longer story, one that involved her whole life in the Chilcotin, that most beautiful and romantic of regions. The Chilcotin lies between the Fraser River on the east and the Coast Mountains on the west. On the north, it is bounded by the endless lodgepole pine forests of the central interior. The mountains cut across its southern boundary, blocking it from the coast and the Fraser River. Much of it is the open rolling ranch country so beloved of wild-west afficionados. It is both cowboy country and the land of the native people, one of the few regions in British Columbia where natives make up half the population. Sparsely populated, much of it was virtually inaccessible except on foot or horseback until the late 1940s, when a road was slowly pushed west from Williams Lake, reaching the coast in 1951. Even that road opened up just a fraction of the Chilcotin. The rest is still the realm of gravel roads, horses and airplanes. It is now and has for many decades been the refuge of people who want to live their lives as unencumbered as possible by the dictates of governments and other people.

Chiwid was born near Redstone in the central Chilcotin in 1903, the daughter of Tsilhqot'in native Loozap and Charlie Skinner, a white horse raiser. Her Tsilhqot'in name meant chickadee; the priest who baptized her gave her the name of Lillie Skinner. Her mother was both deaf and dumb, communicating through sign language. Her father was most at home with the horses he raised and had little to do with his daughter.

Chiwid grew up a serenely beautiful woman; her transcendent beauty would be commented upon almost until she died. She married Alex Jack, a man with a reputation for meanness and violence, and the couple had two daughters. Some who knew them said that Chiwid suffered through many beatings. One day in the late 1930s, Jack inflicted the worst beating of all, using, it was said, a logging chain he flailed at her head. Severely injured, Chiwid was brought out to Williams Lake, then to Vancouver. When she returned to the Chilcotin, she chose a completely different way of life. For the next four decades, she lived alone and outdoors.

Chiwid was known to many in the Chilcotin, who respected her nomadic ways.[5] She first came to the attention of the outside world in 1959, when an RCMP constable from Alexis Creek and a provincial game warden were summoned in the cold of January to help search for someone who had been reported calling out in distress somewhere near Tatla Lake, a hamlet halfway between Williams Lake and Bella Coola. They found no one seeking help, but they did find Chiwid. The constable reported in the RCMP quarterly magazine that Chiwid—he called her the Cattle Queen, for the small herd of cattle that she tended—was middle-aged and had married children who lived on Indian reserves. She did not want to live with them, though, choosing instead a life of total seclusion. They had found her in a pine-bough enclosure in what they called a "desolate area," one that perhaps seemed less desolate to those used to living in the forest. "She had no blankets or warm clothing of any kind. The only clothing she had at all was what she had on her back—a tattered dress and sweater that wouldn't have covered an eight-year-old child."[6] In her shelter were her bedding, some dried moosemeat, ten rabbits, a grouse, a little sugar, some lard and her few personal possessions, including an old .22 rifle.

For the next two decades, Chiwid continued to fascinate the outside world. Young *Vancouver Sun* reporter Paul St. Pierre, who would become known as the chronicler of

Chilcotin life, went looking for Chiwid in the autumn of 1959. He never found her, but he did gather together some of the details of her life. Those who knew her told him Chiwid wore a stocking cap, black woollen stockings, moccasins, a skirt and a man's coat that a storekeeper at Anahim Lake had given her. But she took nothing for free; two days after she received the coat, she dragged a sack of moose meat to the store in payment.

St. Pierre discovered what the people of the Chilcotin had long known about Chiwid. She ranged from Nimpo Lake to Big Creek to Nemiah, over many square miles of wilderness and ranchland. She shot squirrels with her .22 rifle, ate the meat and sold the skins as long as there was a market for them. A dead accurate shot, she also used her old rifle with the home-made sight to shoot larger game such as deer, and sometimes even moose. She snared rabbits and grouse with string snares; she netted fish at creek mouths or in the lakes. She thought nothing of wading into an ice-cold lake to her waist.

When Chiwid had cattle, she grazed them where she could find a narrow strip of grass, then moved them to another, carrying her belongings, piece by piece, on her back to the new meadow. She cut winter hay for them with a knife. Eventually, she sold the cattle, or they died. For many years, she led an old black horse, but it died of starvation one winter. Only Chiwid could survive the kind of life she led.

She always camped outside, beside a small fire that she fed with sticks and twigs. Sometimes she dug into the ground, lit a fire, then swept away the ashes and slept on the warm ground. If she carried a tent, as some said she did, she never used it. Instead, she built a windbreak of evergreen boughs and draped a small tarpaulin over it. In its shelter, she sat or slept in blankets and layers of clothes. There, she cooked her small supply of food and drank tea from her tiny stock of flour, sugar, tea and rice. She followed a nomadic life, even more than the old traditions of the Tsilhqot'in dictated, digging wild potatoes in the Potato Mountains as her people had for centuries, picking berries, fishing, hunting, trapping and drying meat. She carried with her just a can or two for making tea and a frying pan, though some stories tell that she cooked her meat over the open fire.

She hated to go inside, even in the coldest weather when the temperature dropped to minus forty and the snow was deep throughout the Chilcotin. Some saw her empty her moccasins of snow, but somehow her feet never froze. Tempted inside on rare occasions, she found, ironically, that she could not get warm, no matter how hot the room. Within a night or two, she fled back to her nomadic outdoor life.

Fourteen years after her first appearance in the *Vancouver Sun*, another reporter caught up with her. "She is a merry-eyed old lady," wrote Dave Stockand in 1973, "with a face like a burnished chunk of mahogany. She has weathered with the country, not aged with it. She is ageless. Her garments are a ragbag of castoffs and her moccasins are in tatters with

Those who speak of Chiwid praise the beauty that endured despite the life she led alone and outdoors. This photograph was taken at one of her simple camps in the Chilcotin. (PHOTO BY AND COURTESY OF VEERA BONNER)

campfire streaks of black. Yet here she prevails and has prevailed for 20 years and perhaps much longer, though she should have been winter-killed long ago."[7]

Paul St. Pierre caught the contradictions of Chiwid's life. "Some people say that Chee Wit should be put in an institution. Most believe that she would have died like a caged bird long ago if that had happened.... Somewhere in the whispering pines or by some lonely meadow she crouches over the flame of a handful of twigs, a little creature who has taken the cruellest blows of man and nature and remained undefeated. I can never again see a winter chickadee without thinking of her."[8]

Some in the Chilcotin said her spirit was allied to that of a coyote. She said herself that she would die only when all the coyotes died. Even when age robbed her of her sight and she moved to be near her daughter on the Stone Reserve, she still preferred to stay outside, not in the warm house where she was always cold. She died in 1986, aged eighty-three, survivor of more than fifty years of living exactly as she wanted.

Notes:
[1] Lawrence, Guy. *Forty Years on the Telegraph Trail* (Quesnel: Carryall Books, 1990), p. 40.
[2] *Victoria Times*, April 27, 1963.
[3] *Whitehorse Star*, August 31, 1928.
[4] Letter to the Editor, *True West*, 1972, as quoted in *Pioneer Days in British Columbia* (Surrey: Heritage House, 1975) Vol. 2, p. 145.
[5] The memories of many, native and non-native, who knew Chiwid, were collected by Sage Birchwater for *Chiwid* (Vancouver: New Star Books, 1995).
[6] as quoted in *The British Columbian*, January 16, 1960.
[7] *Vancouver Sun*, June 26, 1973.
[8] *Vancouver Sun*, September 5, 1959.

EVERY OUNCE OF
SHOCK AND DRAMA

Words from
the Hinterland

One September day in 1927, Else Lübcke descended from the train that had brought her from Montreal to Vancouver, the last leg of her long journey from Berlin. She crossed the street to the St. Francis Hotel, went to the room reserved for her, and began to unpack. A knock sounded on the door. She opened it to meet George Seel, a Bavarian immigrant of fifteen years standing, a trapper and prospector from north-central British Columbia.

They had never met before, exchanging just a few letters between Berlin and Ootsa Lake. But George was a ruggedly handsome man with a life that Europeans thought romantic, and for Else, adventure and romance were aphrodisiac enough. They walked between the small wooden houses to the beach, they talked, they ate dinner. The next day, they got married. A few days later, they took the steamer north, bound for George's small cabin in the lakes country between Prince Rupert and Prince George.

Seel's tale might have been lost in the wilderness, just one more story of a mail-order bride and hardship in tough times, except for one thing. Else Lübcke Seel was a writer, part of the literary set in Berlin. In the British Columbia north, she continued her literary life, devouring every publication that was sent to her, lining her cabin walls with books by Schopenhauer and Nietzsche, and writing a diary, poems, short stories, songs and articles for German periodicals. For ten years after World War II, she corresponded with Ezra Pound, becoming his guide to German culture and establishing a unique connection between an unknown immigrant writer in the Canadian wilderness and a famed and disgraced American poet locked up in an institution for the criminally insane.

Else was born in 1894 in Pomerania, an area now part of Poland. The family was well off, but her father died when she was seven, and World War I and its aftermath impoverished them. She moved with her mother and aunt to Berlin,

A young Else Lübcke in the mountains before she left Germany for the uncertain life of a trapper's wife in the northern wilderness. (UNIVERSITY OF VICTORIA SPECIAL COLLECTIONS)

where she supported the trio by clipping foreign newspapers for a bank. A strong, independent and lively woman, she wrote short stories and articles and became part of the thriving Berlin literary scene—a scene Seel's translator, Rodney Symington, describes as "a cultural effervescence in which movements, tendencies, and individuals alike were able to flourish in an atmosphere of freedom that bordered on licence."[1]

That atmosphere allowed her temporary escape from the bonds imposed on her by living with two elderly female relatives, but she could not make up her mind to a more permanent escape, and possibly a more permanent captivity, through marriage. Then, in her late twenties, she fell desperately in love with a visiting Danish writer. "Europe lies at his feet," she wrote of her lover, "and he lies at my feet."[2] But not for long. Predictably, he treated her badly and returned to his wife in Denmark.

The rejection intensified Else's belief that old-world Europe was crowded, regimented, tired and sullied by petty betrayals. In comparison, the Canadian wilderness must have seemed new, fresh, clean and open. We can only guess at the combined excitement and trepidation she must have felt when she read in one of her papers an advertisement from a prospector and trapper—those most romantic of occupations—who lived in the western Canadian wilderness—that most romantic of locations. She replied immediately. Not long after, in a fine symbolic gesture, she cut off her long hair and laid it and a ticket to Canada on the table in front of her mother.

A few months later, the Seels stood by the rail of a steamer headed north, he tall, powerfully built, with brown wavy hair and an intelligent cheerful face, she slight, more vivacious than beautiful, dressed in stylish European clothes. At Prince Rupert they took the train east, to an area opened up for settlement just a decade earlier with the completion of the railway from Prince George to Prince Rupert. From Burns Lake they headed south by truck and boat into a region where long, finger-like lakes stretched between rolling hills towards the mountains and the forests.

Else found Ootsa Lake a "particularly Canadian vista," with its huge expanse of water, evergreen forests and snow-covered mountains. At their destination, George lifted her out of the boat and carried her through the doorway of his raw and unfinished two-room cabin. She unpacked her fine linen, china and glass, but George declared them too fancy for Ootsa. She kept out only her Pomeranian feather bedding, the few necessaries and her beloved books. She

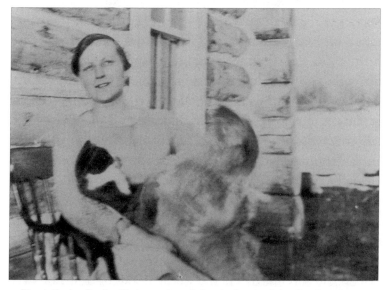

Else Lübcke Seel with her cat and dog in front of the Seel's cabin near Ootsa Lake in north-central British Columbia. (UNIVERSITY OF VICTORIA SPECIAL COLLECTIONS)

scrubbed her first laundry on a washboard, bringing forth from George the comment, "Here for the first time since the earth was born hangs the wash."[3]

A week after they arrived at Ootsa, Else was alone. With George away for two months trapping and hunting, she began to learn the reality of life in the wilderness. She did not know how to light a fire, make biscuits or bake bread. The simplest domestic skills were unknown to her. She listened to coyotes howl, she got her water in a pail from the lake, and she ran from her cabin to the distant neighbours when native people arrived on the shore. The neighbours made light of her fears, but "unfortunately," she noted, "I had read too many horror stories of their supposed activities."[4]

George returned from his trip with mink, marten, ermine and lynx skins. The money from his catch bought staples to see them through the winter and gas for their outboard motor. The temperature dropped to minus forty. Else adapted to a settler's routine, broken by George's comings and goings and by the occasional concert or dance in the community hall, where she delighted in the flirtatious attention paid to her, and, it would seem, in the disapproval of other women at the dance. She made friends with others in the region, though her poor English and intellectualism made her feel deeply isolated from her neighbours.

She read avidly anything that came her way: Canadian newspapers, American magazines, English-language books, German publications sent to her by friends in Germany. She wrote poetry and prose, including articles for German newspapers, such as one defending women of the Canadian north against disparaging remarks made by a travelling German journalist. She had no wish to return to the softer life of the more civilized continent she had fled. Her loneliness when he was gone made her all the more eager for the love and company of her adventuresome husband. When George came home for the second time, they had a "splendid merry-go-round" of love-making, cooking meals and talking. The wild geese flew over the lake and Else was one with them in spirit: "It's always the same; being locked up corrupts everything that is powerful, fresh and happy. In the far distance, I see thousands trotting to work in the morning. Once I belonged to them; today I've lost that kind of submission; here will I stay, live and die."[5]

Pregnant, she took the train to Prince Rupert, followed by a little tourist trip up the coast and over to the Queen Charlotte Islands, taking notes all the while for articles she would write. Back home, George declared that he had found great prospects for a silver mine, and a mining engineer came north to start work. When the mine closed for the winter, the engineer wrote big cheques for everyone involved. In November, she travelled to Hazelton to have her baby in the hospital there, the doctor in Burns Lake having decamped because the local people were too poor to pay him.

The baby made no difference to George's wanderings, but the wanderings made no difference to Else's feeling for the land, which deepened as time went on. "Gradually," she wrote, "I get into a strange mood. Everything seems absurd to me. The newspaper I read, the letters from Europe, my mother's descriptions of her visits, the Steiglitz park with its flowerbeds, all become a boundless nothing. Here I walk across our land, wildflowers and weeds cover it; fallen, fossilized tree trunks, whose roots still rear up into the air, young poplars and willows, tall fir trees and bushes, and in the highest tree an eagle's eyrie…. I love this piece of earth, every stone, every wave, rain and sun, ducks and moon."[6]

In 1929, George Seel sold half his share in the mine and presented Else with $1,000 so she and their baby son could go back to Germany for a visit. The money and the mine marked the high point of their life at Ootsa. When she returned, everything had changed. The depression had hit northern British Columbia, the mine had closed, wheat was worth little and furs even less. While she was gone, George had lent out much of his money; it would never be seen again. Then George was badly burned in an accident miles from home.

Else, pregnant again, contemplated what seemed to be her inevitable fate. "I, too, once dreamed of fame, but I have renounced this dream, my life has become small, the life of all, without importance, and I have chosen the vocation of all women: bearing children. Yet I remain unperturbed, for I wanted this life, the small life, since one must be called to a big one…. [I am] not better or cleverer than other women,"[7] she wrote, though once she had believed she was.

Somehow, they scraped the money together for another trip to the Hazelton hospital, and a daughter was born. Ever tied to her past intellectual life, Else read a biography of King Charles XII of Sweden as she waited for the birth.

The Seels tried to start a beaver farm, but the enterprise—which took much hard work—was doomed. "I toiled to feed the beavers," she wrote, "sank above my thighs in the snow, shoveled the door free and a path to the beaver-lodges, and dragged poplar trees over to the beaver-tank, sweat broke out all over me because of the effort, and tears ran down my cheeks, but they froze in the bitter cold. That made me realize clearly how senseless it was to cry."[8]

She realized now the meaning of marriage, the staying together through thick and thin. Yet her belief in George was fraying. Now that she must experience its effects, she saw the downside of the wandering wilderness life that Germans had romanticized. He was a dreamer, she thought, always on the move, always seeking that elusive gold or silver mine, never giving thought to what his restlessness meant to his family. He was not demonstrative; she treasured each all-too-rare sign of his love. She managed to extract a few scarce dollars from her German savings account, but George packed up most of the fat, flour and gasoline that the money bought and disappeared on yet another prospecting trip. "Is he a fool or am I? Oh God we are two toilsome and burdened people, and have to pull at one string. Sometimes it becomes so hard that I cry, like today, but no one sees it."[9]

In 1932, George earned a total of $69.50. Proud and unbending, he refused to go on relief and go to work at a camp as did many other men in the district. A friend, a man from Berlin who lived in the neighbourhood, killed himself. Too late, Else realized he had wanted to talk to her, a fellow German and a person who might understand, about his homosexual urges. Yet her children delighted her, and when George finally took her on her first wilderness trip in 1935, all the old magic surged again. She wrote long poetic descriptions of this domain of the trapper and a sadly descriptive saga of the now-failed mine.

The 1930s rolled on. Once the children went to school, Seel grew fond of her solitude, thinking and writing alone in her cabin, having long bilingual conversations with herself, reading history, making friends with the poets and philosophers who lived in her books. And then the war came.

Battered by the anti-German propaganda that poured from the radio, Seel soon sensed a cooling of some of the friendships that had sustained her. "The neighbours will turn against us," she predicted, "and antagonize me with bitter accusations and I am powerless to answer back."[10] One evening, as she walked home with her daughter, Gloria, a shot sounded and a bullet whistled by her cheek—and then another. Gloria threw herself down on the ground, but Seel was too furious to be afraid. She ran through the bush towards the culprits, shouting that they were cowards and demanding that they show themselves. They did not, but she knew who they were: sons and nephews of the man who had been her first friend at Ootsa.

The sadnesses mounted up. Her brother was killed in the war. The son of a close friend died at Stalingrad. A close friend and neighbour, a ceaseless complainer, killed herself. "Ootsa blew into your eyes,/Drove you to excess," wrote Seel. "Poor woman, she was superficial and indifferent; she did not wish to be responsible for anything; this lonely life was beyond her strength."[11] But it was not beyond Else Seel's strength.

Towards the end of the war, news arrived from Germany that the invading Russians and Poles had hacked her old writing desk to pieces and burned the books, papers and pictures she had left behind. Ill, Seel took to her bed, where she read and wrote surrounded by her precious books. But the war and its aftermath brought prosperity back to Ootsa. Tourists came to stay in cabins the Seels built, and both George and son Rupert had steady work. In a magazine that came by mail, Seel read of Ezra Pound. The groundbreaking American poet had cast his lot on the wrong side, creating and broadcasting Fascist and anti-Semitic propaganda from Italy. To save the embarrassment of a trial for treason, the American courts had committed him to an insane asylum. Seel wrote to him, sending him news and a pair of moccasins. The correspondence continued for many years, as Seel interpreted German culture for Pound, and Pound, in terse notes, asked her for ever more information and made suggestions for her own research and writing.

Then more bad news arrived. To provide power for the new aluminum plant at Kitimat on the coast, engineers planned to turn the waters of the finger lakes around, funneling them towards a new power plant. The flood waters from the dam would back up over half their land, inundating their cabin, their barn, their garden and their neighbours' property. "Nothing would remain of our life and work—nothing."[12] She and George decided they would not stay to see the devastation: they would move to the nearby Nadina River and start a cattle ranch.

The winter of 1950 was a terrible one for George; prospecting for a mining company, he lived at minus forty-five in miserable conditions and returned little more than a skeleton. Late in March, he died without warning of a heart attack. Devastated, Seel sold the cows, leased the meadows that would not be flooded and fled to Victoria, where her daughter was attending teachers' college. She came back once more, to finish her business with Ootsa. As she left for the last time, it began to snow. "Did the sky," she asked, "...wish to cover our wounds with snow?"[13] In 1952, she wrote once more to Pound. What shall I do, she asked. "Can I sit here and drink tea from dainty little dishes and tables for the rest of my life?"[14] And in another letter, "All at once everything falls away, everything is gone—no husband, no children, no nothing.... What shall I do? Blow myself to the winds, vanish vamoose? I cannot take a map of the world again like 25 years ago and go to another continent. There is only the intellectual life to fall back on. I learned a lot, have strong impulses, many emotions, and my roots are in the soil and not in hollow, shallow words. I have to come to an end here soon, very soon. Put a match to the house and wish I could burn myself with it like the phoenix—but nix, nix."[15]

By 1954, she had grown annoyed with Ezra Pound, convinced she had been just an amusement for him, a slave to his need for entertainment and contact with those outside his prison, and worried that he had too great an influence over her and her writing. She stopped writing to him in 1956, two years before he was released from the asylum. She travelled to see her daughter, who had married and moved to England, and also went back to continental Europe. She lived out her life in Vancouver, continuing her writing for most of the rest of her life. In 1964, her edited *Canadian Diary* was published in Germany, slightly sensationalized to meet the German hunger for romantic and dramatic accounts of Canadian wilderness life. She died in Vancouver in 1973, a year after Ezra Pound.

❦

Else Lübcke Seel was European, intellectual, internalized, a voice almost unheard in the story of the west. Margaret "Ma" Lally Murray was American, uneducated, brash, noisy, and perhaps the best-known voice of the British Columbia hinterland. Yet the two women shared many traits and experiences. Both were immigrants, though from very different families. Both were independent and determined women. Both left their home countries looking for romance, though they chased and found it in rather different ways.

Both married dreamers, though Seel's dreamer was a man of action who chased golden rainbows and Murray's a thoughtful politician who chased more political ends. Both devoted a large part of their lives to rearing children, though Murray's energy and dash took her away from the family home. And both were writers who lived far from big cities and who found their true expression in what they wrote.

Margaret Lally was born in Kansas in 1888, the seventh of nine children in a Catholic farm family. Known even as a small child for her short temper and colourful language, she described herself as a tomboy. "There was always a tomboy in every family in Kansas," she wrote in the 1930s, explaining why she never had her ears pierced although she wanted to. "It has its advantages, too, when there were dishes to do, but it played a rude trick on me, when just as the piercings got under way, the cows broke out into the cornfield and Maggie was slated to go and drive them out.... Give me a good intelligent hog. You can usually drive him—Could I get those ornery bovine critters out of that cornfield. Not until they chased me all over the south quarter, and when I got back to the quilting the women had all gone home."[16] She didn't take to formal education, leaving school at the age of thirteen with a Grade 3 education after a stormy quarrel with the teacher. She moved to Kansas City, but was intrigued by the idea of the romantic Canadian prairie and set off with her sister a few years later for Seattle, then Vancouver. There, she got a job working for a newspaper run by young publisher George Murray, a dreamer, reader and excellent writer who ran the outspoken Vancouver *Chronicle*. Following a job move to Alberta, she came back to Vancouver for a few days on business and George Murray proposed. They got married the next day.

The early years of the Murrays' married life followed a familiar pattern: pregnancy and financial hardship. By 1916, they had a daughter, Georgina, and a son, Daniel. Hit hard by the financial problems that followed World War II, they lived, said Murray, on bread, soup, rice, porridge and fruit she picked and canned herself. George was ever impractical with any money that did come along, splurging on fancy gifts when the family yearned for better food. But they did manage to find the ten dollars to file on a twenty-acre (eight-hectare) homestead up Burrard Inlet from Vancouver.

In 1919, the Murrays went back to Kansas for a visit, and Margaret took ill, to the point of semi-paralysis; it was the beginning of problems with her legs that would plague her all her life. Back in Canada, the family lived on the stump ranch, where Margaret scooted around the house on a rocking chair until she regained the use of her legs. George was working for wages now. As managing editor of the *Vancouver Sun*, he was better able to feed his family and they moved back to Vancouver.

For the Murrays, the depression of the 1930s began in 1928. Again without work, George, always the promoter of trade with Asia, was hired to go to the Orient to write articles about trade and to promote British Columbia products. Margaret put the kids into boarding school and travelled the province showing rural women how to make comforters and rugs, selling them the tools and materials for their crafts and some of her own crafts on the side.

Always interested in politics, and strongly convinced of the economic potential in British Columbia's hinterland, George got the Liberal nomination for the Lillooet riding in 1933. The original Mile 0 of British Columbia's Cariboo Gold Rush road, Lillooet still maintained the atmosphere of a frontier town: a main street wide enough to turn a span of oxen in, dusty sagebrush hills, fertile irrigated benches high above the Fraser River and the remains of gold-washing operations along the river bars and banks. Westwards, towards the mountains, a new gold rush was underway in the mines and prospects of Bralorne and Bridge River.

Until now somewhat overshadowed by her husband and his rather prissy family, Margaret came into her own in Lillooet. Was George invited to speak at two different places at one time? Margaret went to one and charmed the back-country audience with her zippy orations. Never worried by her lack of education or her natural approach to language, she cursed—though mildly—and spoke in her high-pitched, carrying voice, dealing with hecklers and Conservative infamy with the same aplomb. In her biography of her parents, Georgina Keddell noted, "Mother wrung every ounce of shock and drama out of every situation she was ever in."[17] The campaign was an early testing ground for the approach that would make her famous.

George was elected and, buoyed by all they had learned in their travels in the riding, the Murrays started a weekly newspaper, the *Bridge River Lillooet News*. Then, as now, a newspaper lived from its advertising. The Murrays got what local ads they could, then headed for the Vancouver advertising agencies, with Margaret tackling those that represented liquor companies. She took gold quartz samples to their offices and persuaded them there was money to be made in the Lillooet region from the men who lived and drank there. The next year and the years after that she was back, bearing giant tomatoes, cantaloupes, pieces of quartz, even a hind quarter of pork, as presents to persuade the local ad men that the Lillooet region had great promise. On one occasion, the Murrays took with them some dressed turkeys to present to the ad men. By the time they arrived, the hotel restaurant was closed. The manager's own refrigerator was small, and the turkeys would not survive in the heat of a hotel room. The solution Margaret devised? Tie them together by their necks and hang them out the window. The sea gulls gathered in the morning and the hotel guests were outraged, but the turkeys were still in fine shape—and probably brought in an extra ad or two.

Murray wasn't shy about supporting liquor advertising. "Down here at the *News* office," she wrote in the paper, "our favourite tipple is overproof rum: $1.25 for a mickey. Mix with honey and nutmeg and boiling hot water. And you can get fourteen people smiling, seven people chuckling, and four people slapping their thighs, which is good mileage out of five bits."[18]

It was in those first few years in Lillooet that she developed the straight-on, almost lurid, prose style that would make her famous, as well as the social philosophy of up with the independent little guy, down with the government, that underlay much of what she thought and wrote. She wrote a paean, for example, to seven prospectors killed in a snowslide: "They are entitled to as much honor as men who die in battle. They were heroes of peace times. They were willing to risk their lives in the enterprise upon which they were engaged. No doles for them! No restraining and deadening influence of the relief camp! They did not want soft jobs but preferred to pit their energies against the perils of Motherlode Mountain."[19]

And, "The world wants people who are positive," she lectured her readers, "people who smile and make the best of things. Depressions are caused by these gloomy, stagnant, sour folks, who always see the worst side of a situation. Fear, suspicion, uncertainty and disaster result from the spreading of negative ideas."[20]

She was at her best when she was describing some perilous outback venture. A younger and an older miner went fishing one day in 1934; Murray takes up the story. "Old Timer thought he would give Tenderfoot a little thrill, and he shouted, Boo-uh! There's a bear! Tenderfoot jumped to one side of the trail, and sure enough there was a brown bear and she made a pass at Old Timer for shouting and disturbing the peaceful slumber of her baby. Old Timer was not long in scrambling up the nearest jack pine, and Tenderfoot beat him a close second. Old Timer lost a boot string but made the top limb a little shaky! Tenderfoot was nearest the enchanted spot where the finny beauties jump and frolic in the burbling stream. He had his fishing rod alright but he was thirty feet too high. Old Timer fortunately had his pipe. They sat in the trees for over three hours until Brown Bear Jr. had finished his nap. Yes they saw lots of fish! They had plenty of tackle too, but they met the search party at dusk with a real fish story—alibi."[21]

George was re-elected in 1937, and in July of that year, the Murrays went to China to look at trade possibilities for British Columbia. That same month, the Japanese attacked Beijing and the Sino-Japanese War began. They were in Shanghai in August. Planes dropped shells on the roof opposite their hotel and fifty people were killed in the bombing of a hotel they had been staying in. George returned from a sortie covered in bloody foam and tissue. He had slipped from the sidewalk into a dead man's chest cavity. They survived, but were out of cash in a city living on cash only. Desperate, they managed to get space on a departing British troop ship, and fled from China to Hong Kong.

When Margaret got back to Lillooet, she pledged she would stay there for the rest of her life. In 1939, the couple got an invitation to meet with the touring King George and Queen Elizabeth. She knitted her own blue costume for the event, but was undecided about how to behave. Her Irish-Catholic heritage suggested she should hate the king, kick him instead of curtsey. But when she saw him, mild and with such a little sword, she began to cry. "I thought of the British gunboat that took us down the Yangtse River," she told a reporter many years later. "And I felt so proud of the British and grateful that instead of curtseying I pumped the King's hand so hard he weaved a bit on the platform."[22]

By the 1940s, Margaret's fair skin had faded in the heat and dryness of the Lillooet country and her short hair had turned to pepper and salt. But her energy hadn't diminished at all and her use of the English language seemed to gain more colour by the year. She peppered her editorials flaying the government with such words as *senile decay*, *panty-waist fortitude*, *meddlesome* and *mischievous*, until her husband asked her what she was trying to do to his political career. But she had taken hold of her role as outspoken newspaper editor and reporter and wouldn't—couldn't—let go.

Early in the 1940s, she went through Edmonton on her way to a Women's Institute convention in Regina and was invigorated by the excitement accompanying the building of the Alaska Highway. She inveigled a pass out of the Northern Alberta Railway to get to Dawson Creek. When she got back to Lillooet, she told her husband that everything he had said, written or thought about the north was absolutely true, and the Alaska Highway would start a boom that would never end. They decided to move north. A year later, they arrived in a Fort St. John that was chaotic with change. From a small outpost in the never-never land of failed crops and dirt-poor settlers, the region had been transformed into a sea of mud churned by American troops and Canadian workers working on the wartime highway. The town was open twenty-four hours a day.

Margaret Murray's career and fame as a plain-speaking spokeswoman for upcountry and common sense germinated in Lillooet. But all of her salty language and George's promoting couldn't make Lillooet into more than it was: a small and dusty town in a hot, dry region whose moment of fame had passed a century before. Fort St. John was different. The Peace might be known as tomorrow country, but the building of the Alaska Highway and the subsequent oil boom drew money, people, and many North American eyes to the region. Her children grown and on their own, Margaret Murray flowered in British Columbia's northeast corner.

It wasn't a simple matter to start a newspaper, since wartime regulations imposed a quota on newsprint. But the Murrays had a paper quota for the small *Howe Sound News* that they ran in tandem with the Lillooet paper. We'll just transfer that quota here, said Margaret—and somehow they got away with it, though for several years the new *Alaska Highway News* also carried a banner that declared it to be the *Howe Sound News*, even though Howe Sound was many miles away and not a word of its goings-on ever appeared in the new paper.

Margaret and George plunged into getting the *News* going. To make friends and garner ads, Margaret did such things as dressing thirty chickens when the butcher was too busy to do so and George took up barbering tools because the barbers in town couldn't cope. Margaret wrote her usual vivid copy—dice weren't thrown, but the ivories galloped—

and printed her not terribly literate correspondents' reports the way they were received.

The Alaska Highway was completed, the Americans and other workers left, and the war ended. The Peace River region hit another slump in cycles of boom and bust. Meanwhile, in Victoria, the Liberals were talking about continuing the political coalition they had entered with the Conservatives at the beginning of the war. Both Murrays saw this as a betrayal, though George's words were somewhat more restrained than Margaret's. We will never be elected again, she told the Liberals, making a prediction that held true for at least another half a century. George decided to run as a Liberal independent in his old riding of Lillooet.

Newspaper owner and writer Margaret (Ma) Murray in front of the old press from the *Alaska Highway News*, ready as ever to promote the Peace River country in words both sharp and colourful.

(Alfred Doucette, Photographer; Fort St. John-North Peace Museum Archives I 988.05.181)

Margaret, meanwhile, made her own plans. Much to the surprise of her husband and family, she declared herself a Social Credit candidate in the Peace River country. The declaration was a shock. Over in next-door Alberta, the Social Credit party, a conservative grass-roots movement with dubious monetary policy, had been in power since 1935 and would remain so until 1971. Margaret had made fun of their ideas in the past—but here she was, running for them. "Personally," George wrote to her from Lillooet, where he had just heard the news, "I would not have been more surprised if you had announced intention to take the Peace River rapids in a barrel."[23] This could, he told her, destroy them all. Other than that, though, he wished her all the best of luck. George was shattered by the thought of what people would think; Margaret never cared what anyone else thought. Even her son's announcement in the Lillooet paper that his mother was related to the rest of the family only by blood could not faze her.

She stumped the Peace River riding, talking fast, well and straightforwardly, never wrapping her opinions up in politicians' language. Though both she and her husband lost the election, her move into politics gave her even more confidence to speak publicly and write prose as direct as anyone could wish for. Ironically, Social Credit would win the next election—and the next and the next, remaining in power in British Columbia until 1974. But Margaret Murray continued her journalistic career, where she probably had more of a stage than she would have had as a politician.

When the Peace exploded with oil excitement in the early 1950s, she became a national figure through a profile in *Chatelaine* magazine. "The rebel queen of the northwest," the writer called her, referring to her by her nickname Ma.

"Cowboys dream of her, miners swear by her, politicians cuss her and everybody loves her," ran the subheads on the story. "Meet Ma Murray, salty sage of the Alaska Highway, and the only woman in Canada to—almost—kick a king."[24] From then on, Margaret was never heard from. Ma Murray reigned.

Though son Dan was to take over the Lillooet paper and daughter Georgina the Fort St. John paper, Margaret, now in her sixties, didn't want to retire. She loved being on centre stage. Dan had come north when Georgina married; after endless rows with his mother, he left again. Meanwhile, George was back in politics, campaigning for the federal riding of the Cariboo, which stretched from central B.C. to the Yukon border. He won and went to Ottawa to battle for better transport, more immigration and increased trade in northern B.C. Though he had much success, he was depressed at the lack of power a federal backbencher wielded and was defeated in the next election.

Ma Murray prepares for one of the television interviews that were second nature to her after years as outspoken newspaper columnist, reporter and salty voice of the hinterland. (FORT ST. JOHN-NORTH PEACE MUSEUM ARCHIVES I 988.01.82)

Ma just kept on going—writing and speaking and fighting and sometimes even winning. "Only flush for No. 2," she harangued when the town faced a water shortage, "curtail bathing to the Saturday night tub, go back to the old washrag, which could always move a lot of B.O. if applied often enough."[25] In an extended metaphor that had more fire than meaning, she wrote, "When a Government's hand is in a dog's mouth, that hand cannot hit at anything very hard."[26] And she never ceased to rail at the city folk, who conspired to keep the hinterland down. Taking aim at the consumer price index, she hearkened back to the good old days before its birth and turned her editorial into fine nostalgia. Those were the times, she wrote,

> before the city took over; the good old days before falsies were invented; before your girlfriend used lipstick; before the page ads were given over to summer sales of panties;…before the girls went for smoking cigarettes; before the radio blared out singing commercials; before the old age pension, family allowances and free hospitalization; before the age of two cars in every garage and two chickens in every pot.
>
> We can bring the index down if we want to without hurting anyone very much. After all we are not compelled to smoke those cigarettes; drink the coca cola; use the lipstick; guzzle the beer; be a man of distinction; smack the golf ball; waste time at a movie; spend money on your wife's permanent; lay around a cottage at the lakeshore; read the sport pages; read the society pages; read the magazines devoted to romance, legs, detective stories, cookery, mystery and mayhem.

The index is a city-made thing, a monster created to frighten the city mobs. Keep it out of
rural Canada. Let us be thankful for rain, sun and
fertile soil, with or without railway services. Let
us be thankful for the things which still remain
for honest men and women to use for their own
support, and for the glory of God.[27]

For more than forty years, Ma's legs had plagued her.
Now they were getting worse, and it was clear to others that
she could not go on working. But she still didn't want to
retire; this was her life. In 1959, the Murrays produced the
biggest special edition of the newspaper ever—and there
had been many special editions, all geared at getting one
paper or another back into the black. Angry because Dan,
back running the paper, had cancelled the offshoot *Fort
Nelson News* because it wasn't making any money, she rode
the bus north to this muskeg and forest town, staying for five
months and getting out four-page editions. She departed on
a stretcher bound for hospital.

The Murrays left Fort St. John and headed back to
Lillooet, where they had heard that the paper they had once
owned was again for sale. As they tried to decide whether to
buy it back, George ran his car off the road; his injuries sent
him to hospital in Vancouver. He was doing well when it was
discovered that he had cancer. He died in August of 1961.

Now seventy-three, Ma would not give up. In Lillooet,
she went back to running her newspaper, ever sassier, ever
ready to take on politicians and bureaucracies. By the 1970s,
she could no longer handle the work, and once more sold
the paper. She died in Lillooet in 1984, a fine example of a
rebellious woman of the west.

Words from the Hinterland

Notes:

1 Symington, Rodney. "Else Seel: Survival, Assimilation, Alienation," in *The Old World and the New: Literary Perspectives of German-Speaking Canadians*, Walter E. Riedel, ed. (Toronto: University of Toronto Press, 1984), p. 20.

2 Symington, Rodney, translator, from notes made by Else Seel, in the Else Seel collection, University of Victoria Special Collections.

3 Seel, Else Lübcke. *The Last Pioneer: My Canadian Diary* (trans. Rodney Symington, unpublished).

4 Ibid.

5 Ibid.

6 Ibid.

7 Ibid.

8 Ibid.

9 Ibid.

10 Ibid.

11 Ibid.

12 Ibid.

13 Ibid.

14 Else Seel letter to Ezra Pound, February 27, 1952.

15 Else Seel letter to Ezra Pound, June 13, 1952.

16 *Bridge River Lillooet News*, March 7, 1935.

17 Keddell, Georgina. *The Newspapering Murrays* (Toronto: McClelland & Stewart, 1967), p. 90.

18 Ibid., p. 94.

19 *Bridge River Lillooet News*, April 11, 1935.

20 Ibid., December 13, 1934.

21 Ibid., June 28, 1934.

22 *Chatelaine*, May, 1952.

23 as quoted in Keddell, *The Newspapering Murrays*, p. 157.

24 *Chatelaine*, May, 1952.

25 as quoted in Keddell, *The Newspapering Murrays*, p. 213.

26 *Alaska Highway News*, January 24, 1952.

27 *Alaska Highway News*, August 9, 1951.

BIBLIOGRAPHY

Books

Andersen, Marnie. *Women of the West Coast, Then and Now*. Sidney: Sand Dollar Press, 1993.

Birchwater, Sage. *Chiwid*. Vancouver: New Star Books, 1995.

Blanchet, M. Wylie. *The Curve of Time*. Vancouver: Whitecap Books, 1990.

Blanchard, Paula. *The Life of Emily Carr*. Vancouver: Douglas and McIntyre, 1988.

Bonner, Veera, et al. *Chilcotin: Preserving Pioneer Memories*. Surrey: Heritage House, 1995.

Cameron, Agnes Deans. *The New North: An Account of a Woman's 1908 Journey through Canada to the Arctic*. Saskatoon: Western Producer Prairie Books, revised edition, 1986.

Campbell, Robert. *Two Journals of Robert Campbell: 1808-1853*. Seattle, Wash.: Limited Edition, n.p. 1958.

Carr, Emily. *Hundreds and Thousands: The Journals of Emily Carr*. Toronto: Clarke, Irwin and Company, 1966.

Carr, Emily. *Growing Pains: The Autobiography of Emily Carr*. Toronto: Clarke, Irwin and Company, 1946, 1966.

Cheadle, Walter. *Cheadle's Journal of a Trip Across Canada, 1862-1863*. Edmonton: M.G. Hurtig Ltd., 1971.

Converse, Cathy. *Mainstays: Women Who Shaped British Columbia*. Victoria: Horsdal and Schubart, 1998.

Creese, Gillian, and Strong-Boag, Veronica, ed. *British Columbia Reconsidered: Essays on Women*. Vancouver: Press Gang, 1992.

Dickinson, Christine Frances, and Smith, Diane Solie. *Atlin: the Story of British Columbia's Last Gold Rush*. Atlin: Atlin Historical Society, 1995.

Douglas, Gilean. *River for my Sidewalk*. Victoria: Sono Nis, 1984.

Douglas, Gilean. *Silence Is My Homeland: Life on Teal River*. Harrisburg, Penn.: Stackpole Books, 1978.

Downie, Jill. *A Passionate Pen: the Life and Times of Faith Fenton*. Toronto: HarperCollins, 1996.

Bibliography

Downs, Art, ed. *Pioneer Days in British Columbia, Vol. 2.* BC Outdoors, 1975.

Dufferin, Lady Hariot. *My Canadian Journal.* Gladys Chantler Walker, ed. Toronto: Longmans Canada, 1969.

Farrow, Moira, *Nobody Here but Us: Pioneers of the North.* Vancouver: J.J. Douglas, 1975.

First History of Rossland. Rossland: Stunden & Perin, 1897.

Fraser, Agnes, writing as Frances Macnab. *British Columbia for Settlers: its mines, trade and agriculture.* London: Chapman & Hall, 1898.

Fredrickson, Olive, with Ben East. *Silence of the North.* Toronto: General Publishing, 1972.

Gould, Jan. *Women of British Columbia.* Saanich: Hancock House, 1975.

Graham, Donald. *Lights of the Inside Passage.* Madeira Park: Harbour Publishing, 1986.

Harris, Lorraine. *Halfway to the Goldfields: A History of Lillooet.* Vancouver: J.J. Douglas, 1977.

Henshaw, Julia. *Why Not Sweetheart.* Toronto: George N. Morang, 1902.

Horsfield, Margaret. *Cougar Annie's Garden.* Nanaimo: Salal Books, 1999.

In the Western Mountains: Early Mountaineering in British Columbia. Victoria: Provincial Archives, 1980.

Jackson, Dr. Mary Percy, *Suitable for the Wilds: Letters from Northern Alberta, 1929-1931.* Toronto: University of Toronto Press, 1995.

Jeffrey, Julie Roy. *Frontier Women: Civilizing the West? 1840-1880.* New York: Hill and Wang, 1998.

Johnston, Lukin. *Beyond the Rockies.* Toronto: J.M. Dent & Sons, 1929.

Keddell, Georgina. *The Newspapering Murrays.* Toronto: McClelland & Stewart, 1967.

Keller, Betty. *Pauline: A Biography of Pauline Johnson.* Vancouver: Douglas & McIntyre, 1981.

Kennedy, Ian. *Sunny Sandy Savary: a History of Savary Island, 1792-1992.* Vancouver: Kennell Publishing, 1992.

Lawrence, Guy. *Forty Years on the Telegraph Trail.* Quesnel: Caryall Books, 1990.

Lebowitz, Andrea, and Milton, Gillian. *Gilean Douglas: Writing Nature, Finding Home.* Victoria: Sono Nis, 1999.

Ludditt, Fred. *Barkerville Days.* Vancouver: Mitchell Press, 1969.

McGregor, J.G. *Paddle Wheels to Bucket Wheels on the Athabasca.* Toronto: McClelland and Stewart Limited, 1974

McRaye, Walter. *Pauline Johnson and Friends.* Toronto: Ryerson Press, 1947.

Munday, Don. *The Unknown Mountain* (introduction by Angus M. Gunn). Lake Louise: Coyote Books, 1993.

Parent, Milton. *Silent Shores and Sunken Ships*. Nakusp: Arrow Lakes Historical Society, 1997.

Patenaude, Bronwen. *Trails to Gold*. Victoria: Horsdal and Schubart, 1995.

Patenaude, Bronwen. *Trails to Gold II: Roadhouses of the Cariboo*. Surrey: Heritage House, 1996.

Patterson, R.M. *Trail to the Interior*. Victoria: Horsdal and Schubart, 1993.

Penrose, Evelyn. *Adventure Unlimited: A Water Diviner Travels the World*. London: Neville Spearman, 1958.

Petersen, Eugene (Pelle). *Window in the Rock*. Fairfield, Wash.: Ye Galleon, 1993.

Raincoast Chronicles, 6/10: Stories and History of the B.C. Coast. Madeira Park: Harbour Publishing, 1983.

Ramsay, Bruce. *Ghost Towns of British Columbia*. Vancouver: Mitchell Press, 1963.

Robideau, Henri. *Flapjacks and Photographs: A History of Mattie Gunterman*. Vancouver: Polestar, 1995.

Skelton, Robin. *They Call It the Cariboo*. Victoria: Sono Nis, 1980.

Smith, Cyndi. *Off the Beaten Track: Women Adventurers and Mountaineers in Western Canada*. Jasper: Coyote Books, 1989.

Spilsbury, Jim, and White, Howard. *Spilsbury's Coast*. Madeira Park: Harbour Publishing, 1987.

Stanwell-Fletcher, Theodora. *Driftwood Valley: a Woman Naturalist in the Northern Wilderness*. Corvallis, Ore.: Oregon State University Press, 1999.

Steele, Peter. *Atlin's Gold*. Prince George: Caitlin Press, 1995.

Storrs, Monica. *Companions of the Peace: Diaries and Letters of Monica Storrs, 1931-1939*. Vera K. Fast, ed. Toronto: University of Toronto Press, 1999.

Storrs, Monica. *God's Galloping Girl: The Peace River Diaries of Monica Storrs, 1929-1931*. W.L. Morton, ed. Vancouver: UBC Press, 1979.

Tippett, Maria. *Emily Carr: A Biography*. Toronto: Stoddart, 1979.

Webber, Jean. *A Rich and Fruitful Land: the History of the Valleys of the Okanagan, Similkameen and Shuswap*. Madeira Park: Harbour Publishing, 1999.

Wright, Richard Thomas, *Barkerville: Williams Creek, Cariboo, a Gold-Rush Experience*. Williams Lake: Winter Quarters Press, 1998.

Bibliography

Pamphlets, Articles and Unpublished Sources

Byron, LaVonne. "The Better Halves: The Way of Life and Influence of Women in the Vernon Area from Settlement to 1921," Okanagan Historical Society Annual Report, Vol. 45.

Carr, Emily. "Nootka Had a Hotel," BCA Emily Carr collection, MG 30, D 215, Vol. 11.

Douglas, Gilean. *A February Face* (unfinished autobiography in the Gilean Douglas collection, Special Collections, University of British Columbia).

Duckworth, Elisabeth. "Tranquille Sanatorium," Kamloops Museum and Archives paper, July 24, 1990.

Homan, Dora, collection, Quesnel and District Museum and Archives.

Red Book of Rossland: Texas Steer Grand Opening, n.p., n.d.

Report of P.S. Lampman, Commissioner, re South Park School Drawing Books, Feb. 23, 1906.

Seel, Else Lübcke. *The Last Pioneer: My Canadian Diary*. Rodney Symington, trans. (unpublished).

Symington, Rodney. "Else Seel: Survival, Assimilation, Alienation," in *The Old World and the New: Literary Perspectives of German-Speaking Canadians*. Walter E. Riedel, ed. Toronto: University of Toronto Press, 1984.

Symington, Rodney. "Five Years I Wrote to You," in *Paideuma: A Journal Devoted to Ezra Pound Scholarship*, Vol. 18, #1 and 2.

Newspapers and Magazines

Alaska Highway News

Atlin Claim

BC Studies

Beautiful British Columbia

Bridge River Lillooet News

British Columbia Historical Quarterly

Canadian West

Cariboo Sentinel

Chatelaine

Forestalk

Kelowna Courier

Northern Sentinel

Okanagan Historical Society Annual Report

Rossland Miner

Vancouver Province

Vancouver Sun

Vancouver World

Victoria Colonist (Daily Colonist, Daily British Colonist)

Victoria Daily Times

Whitehorse Star

INDEX

(page numbers in italics indicate photographs)

Index

Index

Index

ABOUT THE AUTHOR

Photo by Anton Studios

ROSEMARY NEERING is definitely a traveller, sometimes an adventurer, and remains in awe of the rebels who challenged the conventions that dictated how women should behave in an earlier time. A writer for all of her adult life, she is happiest when exploring, whether on back roads in the wilds of the west or in the stacks and filing cabinets of libraries and archives.

She is the author of a number of books about the Canadian west, including *Down the Road: Journeys through Small-Town British Columbia* and *A Traveller's Guide to Historic British Columbia,* and co-author of *Over Canada: An Aerial Adventure.* She is a frequent contributor to and contributing editor for *Beautiful British Columbia* magazine.

She lives in Victoria, where she gardens, plays tennis, and spends many hours thinking about her next trip in Canada, South America or Europe.